50 Malaysian Recipes for Home

By: Kelly Johnson

Table of Contents

- Nasi Lemak
- Beef Rendang
- Roti Canai with Curry
- Hainanese Chicken Rice
- Char Kway Teow
- Laksa
- Satay with Peanut Sauce
- Mee Goreng
- Ayam Percik
- Curry Laksa
- Nasi Goreng
- Nasi Kerabu
- Sambal Udang (Spicy Chili Shrimp)
- Assam Pedas
- Murtabak
- Nasi Ayam (Chicken Rice)
- Apam Balik (Malaysian Pancake)
- Lontong
- Mee Rebus
- Kuih Ketayap (Pandan Crepes)
- Penang Hokkien Mee
- Kari Ayam (Chicken Curry)
- Nasi Dagang
- Rojak
- Acar
- Mee Siam
- Prawn Mee
- Otak-Otak
- Ikan Bakar (Grilled Fish)
- Kuih Lapis (Layer Cake)
- Nasi Tomato (Tomato Rice)
- Curry Puff
- Yong Tau Foo
- Kaya Toast
- Nasi Ulam

- Ais Kacang (Shaved Ice Dessert)
- Bubur Cha Cha (Sweet Potato and Tapioca Dessert)
- Kuih Talam (Pandan and Coconut Cake)
- Roti Jala (Lacy Pancakes)
- Laksam
- Bubur Pulut Hitam (Black Glutinous Rice Porridge)
- Soto Ayam (Chicken Soup)
- Ketupat
- Pulut Panggang (Grilled Glutinous Rice)
- Cendol
- Mee Jawa
- Nasi Lemuni
- Sambal Belacan
- Mee Bandung Muar
- Sambal Goreng

Nasi Lemak

Ingredients:

For the Rice:

- 2 cups jasmine rice
- 2 cups coconut milk
- 1 3-inch piece of fresh pandan leaf (optional)
- 1 teaspoon salt

For the Sambal (Spicy Chili Paste):

- 10-12 dried red chilies, soaked in hot water for 15 minutes, drained, and seeded
- 3 shallots, peeled
- 3 cloves garlic, peeled
- 2 tablespoons dried shrimp, soaked in hot water for 10 minutes (optional)
- 2 tablespoons tamarind pulp, soaked in 1/4 cup hot water, strained, and seeds discarded
- 2 tablespoons sugar
- Salt to taste
- 2 tablespoons vegetable oil

For the Accompaniments:

- Hard-boiled eggs, halved
- Fried anchovies (ikan bilis)
- Roasted peanuts
- Sliced cucumber
- Sliced tomato
- Fresh banana leaves, for serving (optional)

Instructions:

1. Rinse the jasmine rice until the water runs clear. Drain well.
2. In a rice cooker or pot, combine the rinsed rice, coconut milk, pandan leaf (if using), and salt. Cook the rice according to your rice cooker's instructions or

bring to a boil, then reduce the heat to low, cover, and simmer for about 15-20 minutes until the rice is cooked and the liquid is absorbed.
3. While the rice is cooking, prepare the sambal. In a blender or food processor, combine the soaked and drained dried red chilies, shallots, garlic, dried shrimp (if using), tamarind paste, sugar, and salt. Blend until you get a smooth paste.
4. Heat the vegetable oil in a skillet or wok over medium heat. Add the blended chili paste and cook, stirring frequently, for about 10-15 minutes until the sambal is thickened and fragrant. Adjust the seasoning with salt and sugar if needed. Remove from heat and set aside.
5. Once the rice is cooked, fluff it with a fork and remove the pandan leaf if used.
6. To serve, place a portion of coconut rice on a plate or banana leaf. Arrange the halved hard-boiled eggs, fried anchovies, roasted peanuts, sliced cucumber, and tomato on the side. Spoon some sambal over the rice.
7. Serve the Nasi Lemak immediately, traditionally wrapped in banana leaves for added fragrance and presentation.
8. Enjoy your delicious and fragrant Nasi Lemak!

Beef Rendang

Ingredients:

- 2 lbs (about 900g) beef chuck, cut into bite-sized pieces
- 4 cups coconut milk
- 2 stalks lemongrass, bruised and tied into knots
- 4 kaffir lime leaves
- 2 turmeric leaves (optional)
- 1 cinnamon stick
- 4 tablespoons tamarind paste
- 3 tablespoons palm sugar or brown sugar
- Salt to taste

For the Spice Paste (Rempah):

- 10 dried red chilies, seeded and soaked in hot water for 15 minutes
- 6 shallots, peeled
- 4 cloves garlic, peeled
- 1 inch ginger, peeled
- 1 inch galangal, peeled
- 1 inch turmeric, peeled
- 2 teaspoons ground coriander
- 1 teaspoon ground cumin
- 1 teaspoon ground fennel
- 1 teaspoon ground turmeric

Instructions:

1. In a blender or food processor, combine all the ingredients for the spice paste (rempeh) and blend until smooth.
2. Heat a large pot or Dutch oven over medium heat. Add the spice paste and cook, stirring frequently, for about 5-7 minutes until fragrant.
3. Add the beef to the pot and cook until browned on all sides, about 5 minutes.
4. Pour in the coconut milk and add the lemongrass, kaffir lime leaves, turmeric leaves (if using), cinnamon stick, tamarind paste, palm sugar, and salt to taste. Stir to combine.
5. Bring the mixture to a boil, then reduce the heat to low. Cover and simmer for 2-3 hours, stirring occasionally, until the beef is tender and the sauce thickens. If the sauce thickens too quickly, add a little water as needed.
6. Once the beef is tender and the sauce has thickened, remove the pot from the heat.

7. Serve the Beef Rendang hot with steamed rice or coconut rice.
8. Enjoy your delicious and aromatic Beef Rendang!

Roti Canai with Curry

Ingredients:

For the Roti Canai:

- 2 cups all-purpose flour
- 1/2 teaspoon salt
- 1 tablespoon sugar
- 1 cup warm water
- 2 tablespoons condensed milk
- 2 tablespoons ghee or butter, melted
- Vegetable oil, for frying

For the Chicken Curry:

- 1 lb (about 450g) chicken thighs, cut into bite-sized pieces
- 2 tablespoons vegetable oil
- 1 onion, chopped
- 2 cloves garlic, minced
- 1 tablespoon ginger, minced
- 2 tablespoons curry powder
- 1 teaspoon turmeric powder
- 1 teaspoon chili powder (optional, adjust to taste)
- 1 cup coconut milk
- 1 cup chicken broth
- 2 potatoes, peeled and diced
- Salt and pepper to taste
- Chopped cilantro for garnish (optional)

Instructions:

1. In a large mixing bowl, combine the all-purpose flour, salt, and sugar. Gradually add the warm water and condensed milk, mixing until a dough forms.
2. Knead the dough on a lightly floured surface for about 5-7 minutes until smooth and elastic. Divide the dough into small balls, about the size of golf balls. Brush each ball with melted ghee or butter, cover with a damp cloth, and let them rest for at least 4 hours or overnight.

3. After resting, flatten each ball with your hands and stretch them into thin, round sheets (similar to making pizza dough). Brush the stretched dough with more melted ghee or butter.
4. Heat a non-stick skillet or griddle over medium heat. Brush with a little vegetable oil. Cook each roti canai for about 2-3 minutes on each side, until golden brown and crispy. Repeat with the remaining dough balls.
5. For the chicken curry, heat vegetable oil in a large skillet or pot over medium heat. Add the chopped onion, garlic, and ginger. Cook until softened and fragrant, about 2-3 minutes.
6. Add the curry powder, turmeric powder, and chili powder (if using). Cook for another 1-2 minutes until the spices are toasted and fragrant.
7. Add the chicken pieces to the skillet and cook until browned on all sides.
8. Pour in the coconut milk and chicken broth. Add the diced potatoes. Bring to a boil, then reduce the heat and let it simmer for about 20-25 minutes until the chicken is cooked through and the potatoes are tender.
9. Season the curry with salt and pepper to taste. Garnish with chopped cilantro if desired.
10. Serve the Roti Canai hot with the chicken curry dipping sauce.
11. Enjoy your delicious Malaysian Roti Canai with Chicken Curry!

Hainanese Chicken Rice

Ingredients:

For the Chicken:

- 1 whole chicken (about 3-4 lbs)
- 4 slices ginger
- 2 stalks spring onions, cut into halves
- Salt, to taste

For the Rice:

- 2 cups jasmine rice
- 2 cups chicken broth (reserved from poaching the chicken)
- 2 cloves garlic, minced
- 2 slices ginger
- 1 pandan leaf (optional)
- Salt, to taste

For the Dipping Sauces:

- Soy sauce
- Chili sauce (store-bought or homemade)
- Ginger paste (finely grated ginger mixed with a little oil and salt)

For Garnish:

- Cucumber slices
- Tomato slices
- Fresh cilantro

Instructions:

1. Rinse the whole chicken under cold running water. Pat dry with paper towels.
2. In a large pot, add enough water to cover the chicken. Add the ginger slices, spring onions, and a pinch of salt. Bring the water to a boil.

3. Carefully lower the chicken into the pot, breast-side down. Bring the water back to a boil, then reduce the heat to low and cover the pot. Let the chicken simmer for about 30-40 minutes, or until cooked through. To check for doneness, insert a chopstick or skewer into the thickest part of the thigh. If the juices run clear, the chicken is cooked.
4. Once the chicken is cooked, remove it from the pot and plunge it into a large bowl of ice water to stop the cooking process. Let it cool completely.
5. Reserve the chicken broth from poaching for cooking the rice.
6. Rinse the jasmine rice until the water runs clear. Drain well.
7. In a rice cooker or pot, add the minced garlic, sliced ginger, pandan leaf (if using), and the rinsed jasmine rice. Add 2 cups of the reserved chicken broth and 2 cups of water (adjust the ratio if needed). Cook the rice according to your rice cooker's instructions or until fluffy and cooked through.
8. While the rice is cooking, prepare the dipping sauces by mixing soy sauce, chili sauce, and ginger paste in separate small bowls.
9. Once the chicken has cooled, chop it into serving pieces. Arrange the chicken pieces on a serving platter.
10. Serve the Hainanese Chicken Rice with the fragrant rice, dipping sauces, cucumber slices, tomato slices, and fresh cilantro.
11. Enjoy your delicious and comforting Hainanese Chicken Rice!

Char Kway Teow

Ingredients:

- 14 oz (about 400g) fresh flat rice noodles
- 8-10 large shrimp, peeled and deveined
- 2 Chinese sausages (lap cheong), sliced thinly
- 2 cloves garlic, minced
- 2 eggs, lightly beaten
- 2 cups bean sprouts
- 2 stalks chives, cut into 2-inch lengths
- 2 tablespoons vegetable oil
- Salt and pepper to taste

For the Sauce:

- 3 tablespoons soy sauce
- 1 tablespoon dark soy sauce
- 1 tablespoon oyster sauce
- 1 tablespoon fish sauce
- 1 tablespoon sweet soy sauce (kecap manis)
- 1 tablespoon chili paste or sambal oelek (optional, adjust to taste)
- 1 teaspoon sugar

Instructions:

1. Soak the fresh flat rice noodles in warm water for about 15-20 minutes to soften them. Drain well and set aside.
2. In a small bowl, mix together all the ingredients for the sauce: soy sauce, dark soy sauce, oyster sauce, fish sauce, sweet soy sauce, chili paste (if using), and sugar. Set aside.
3. Heat 1 tablespoon of vegetable oil in a large wok or skillet over high heat. Add the beaten eggs and scramble until cooked. Remove the eggs from the wok and set aside.
4. In the same wok or skillet, add the remaining tablespoon of vegetable oil. Add the minced garlic and stir-fry until fragrant, about 30 seconds.
5. Add the sliced Chinese sausages to the wok and stir-fry for 1-2 minutes until they start to brown.
6. Add the shrimp to the wok and stir-fry until they turn pink and cooked through.
7. Add the softened rice noodles to the wok, along with the prepared sauce. Use a pair of chopsticks or tongs to toss everything together until well combined.

8. Add the bean sprouts and chives to the wok. Continue to stir-fry for another 2-3 minutes until the noodles are evenly coated in the sauce and the bean sprouts are slightly wilted.
9. Return the scrambled eggs to the wok and toss everything together again.
10. Season the Char Kway Teow with salt and pepper to taste, if needed.
11. Serve the Char Kway Teow hot, garnished with extra bean sprouts and chopped chives if desired.
12. Enjoy your delicious and flavorful Char Kway Teow!

Laksa

Ingredients:

For the Laksa Paste:

- 6 dried red chilies, soaked in hot water for 15 minutes
- 4 shallots, peeled
- 3 cloves garlic, peeled
- 1-inch piece ginger, peeled
- 1-inch piece galangal, peeled
- 1 tablespoon dried shrimp, soaked in hot water for 10 minutes (optional)
- 2 stalks lemongrass, white part only, thinly sliced
- 1 tablespoon ground coriander
- 1 teaspoon ground turmeric
- 1 teaspoon ground cumin
- 1 tablespoon shrimp paste (belacan)
- 2 tablespoons vegetable oil

For the Laksa Broth:

- 4 cups chicken or vegetable broth
- 2 cups coconut milk
- 2 kaffir lime leaves
- 1 tablespoon palm sugar or brown sugar
- 1 tablespoon fish sauce or soy sauce
- Salt to taste

For the Toppings:

- 8 oz (about 225g) rice vermicelli noodles, cooked according to package instructions
- Cooked chicken, shrimp, tofu, fish cake, or any other protein of your choice
- Bean sprouts
- Hard-boiled eggs, halved
- Fresh cilantro leaves
- Lime wedges
- Sambal or chili paste (optional, for extra heat)

Instructions:

1. To make the Laksa paste, drain the soaked dried red chilies and place them in a blender or food processor. Add the shallots, garlic, ginger, galangal, soaked dried shrimp (if using), sliced lemongrass, ground coriander, ground turmeric, ground cumin, and shrimp paste. Blend until you get a smooth paste.
2. Heat the vegetable oil in a large pot over medium heat. Add the Laksa paste to the pot and cook, stirring constantly, for about 5-7 minutes until fragrant.
3. Pour in the chicken or vegetable broth and coconut milk. Add the kaffir lime leaves, palm sugar, and fish sauce or soy sauce. Stir to combine.
4. Bring the Laksa broth to a gentle simmer and let it cook for about 15-20 minutes to allow the flavors to meld together. Taste and adjust the seasoning with salt if needed.
5. While the broth is simmering, prepare your desired toppings by cooking the protein of your choice and any vegetables you'd like to add.
6. To serve, divide the cooked rice vermicelli noodles among serving bowls. Ladle the hot Laksa broth over the noodles.
7. Arrange the cooked protein, bean sprouts, halved hard-boiled eggs, and fresh cilantro leaves on top of the noodles.
8. Serve the Laksa hot, garnished with lime wedges and sambal or chili paste on the side for extra heat.
9. Enjoy your delicious and aromatic Laksa! Adjust the spiciness level by adding more or fewer dried chilies to the Laksa paste according to your preference.

Satay with Peanut Sauce

Ingredients:

For the Satay:

- 1 lb (about 450g) chicken breast or thigh, thinly sliced into strips
- 1 tablespoon soy sauce
- 1 tablespoon fish sauce
- 1 tablespoon brown sugar
- 2 cloves garlic, minced
- 1 teaspoon ground coriander
- 1 teaspoon ground cumin
- 1 teaspoon turmeric powder
- 1 tablespoon vegetable oil
- Bamboo skewers, soaked in water for 30 minutes

For the Peanut Sauce:

- 1 cup roasted unsalted peanuts
- 2 cloves garlic, minced
- 1 shallot, minced
- 1 tablespoon vegetable oil
- 1 tablespoon brown sugar
- 1 tablespoon soy sauce
- 1 tablespoon tamarind paste dissolved in 1/4 cup warm water (or substitute with lime juice)
- 1 teaspoon ground coriander
- 1 teaspoon ground cumin
- 1/2 teaspoon chili powder (adjust to taste)
- 1 cup coconut milk
- Salt to taste

Instructions:

1. In a bowl, combine the thinly sliced chicken with soy sauce, fish sauce, brown sugar, minced garlic, ground coriander, ground cumin, turmeric powder, and vegetable oil. Mix well to coat the chicken evenly. Cover and marinate in the refrigerator for at least 1 hour, or overnight for best results.

2. While the chicken is marinating, prepare the peanut sauce. In a blender or food processor, blend the roasted peanuts until they form a coarse powder.
3. Heat vegetable oil in a saucepan over medium heat. Add the minced garlic and shallot, and cook until softened and fragrant, about 2-3 minutes.
4. Add the ground coriander, ground cumin, and chili powder to the saucepan. Cook for another minute until the spices are toasted and fragrant.
5. Add the ground peanuts to the saucepan, along with brown sugar, soy sauce, tamarind paste (or lime juice), and coconut milk. Stir to combine.
6. Bring the peanut sauce to a gentle simmer, then reduce the heat to low. Let it cook for about 10-15 minutes, stirring occasionally, until the sauce thickens slightly. If the sauce is too thick, you can add more coconut milk or water to reach your desired consistency. Season with salt to taste.
7. Preheat the grill or grill pan over medium-high heat.
8. Thread the marinated chicken strips onto the soaked bamboo skewers.
9. Grill the chicken skewers for about 3-4 minutes on each side, or until cooked through and slightly charred.
10. Serve the grilled chicken skewers hot with the peanut sauce on the side for dipping.
11. Enjoy your delicious Satay with Peanut Sauce as an appetizer or main dish!

Mee Goreng

Ingredients:

- 12 oz (about 340g) yellow noodles
- 2 tablespoons vegetable oil
- 2 cloves garlic, minced
- 1 small onion, thinly sliced
- 1 small carrot, julienned
- 1 bell pepper, thinly sliced
- 1 cup cabbage, thinly sliced
- 1 cup bean sprouts
- 8 oz (about 225g) shrimp, peeled and deveined (optional)
- 2 eggs, lightly beaten
- 2 tablespoons soy sauce
- 1 tablespoon sweet soy sauce (kecap manis)
- 1 tablespoon tomato ketchup
- 1 tablespoon chili paste or sambal oelek (adjust to taste)
- 1 tablespoon lime juice
- Salt and pepper to taste
- Chopped green onions and cilantro for garnish
- Lime wedges for serving

Instructions:

1. Cook the yellow noodles according to the package instructions. Drain and set aside.
2. Heat the vegetable oil in a large wok or skillet over medium-high heat. Add the minced garlic and sliced onion, and stir-fry for about 1 minute until fragrant.
3. Add the julienned carrot, sliced bell pepper, and sliced cabbage to the wok. Stir-fry for 2-3 minutes until the vegetables are slightly softened.
4. Push the vegetables to one side of the wok and add the beaten eggs to the empty side. Scramble the eggs until cooked through, then mix them with the vegetables.
5. Add the cooked shrimp (if using) to the wok and stir-fry until pink and cooked through.
6. Add the cooked yellow noodles and bean sprouts to the wok. Toss everything together until well combined.
7. In a small bowl, mix together the soy sauce, sweet soy sauce, tomato ketchup, chili paste, and lime juice. Pour the sauce over the noodles and toss to coat evenly.
8. Season the Mee Goreng with salt and pepper to taste. Adjust the seasoning or add more chili paste if you prefer it spicier.
9. Continue to stir-fry for another 2-3 minutes until everything is heated through and well combined.
10. Garnish the Mee Goreng with chopped green onions and cilantro.

11. Serve hot with lime wedges on the side for squeezing over the noodles.
12. Enjoy your delicious and spicy Mee Goreng! Adjust the ingredients and spice level according to your taste preferences.

Ayam Percik

Ingredients:

For the Chicken:

- 1 whole chicken, cut into pieces or chicken thighs and drumsticks
- 2 tablespoons tamarind paste
- 2 tablespoons water
- Salt to taste

For the Spice Paste:

- 6 shallots, peeled
- 4 cloves garlic, peeled
- 2 stalks lemongrass, white part only, thinly sliced
- 1 inch ginger, peeled
- 1 inch galangal, peeled
- 4-6 dried red chilies, soaked in hot water and seeded
- 1 teaspoon ground turmeric
- 1 teaspoon ground coriander
- 1 teaspoon ground cumin
- 1 tablespoon brown sugar
- 1 tablespoon vegetable oil

For the Coconut Gravy:

- 1 cup coconut milk
- 2 tablespoons tamarind paste
- 2 tablespoons water
- 1 tablespoon brown sugar
- Salt to taste

Instructions:

1. In a small bowl, mix together the tamarind paste and water. Rub the chicken pieces with the tamarind mixture and a pinch of salt. Let them marinate for at least 30 minutes, or preferably overnight in the refrigerator.
2. In a blender or food processor, combine all the ingredients for the spice paste: shallots, garlic, lemongrass, ginger, galangal, soaked dried red chilies, ground turmeric, ground coriander, ground cumin, brown sugar, and vegetable oil. Blend until you get a smooth paste.
3. Preheat the grill or oven to medium-high heat.
4. Grill or roast the marinated chicken pieces until cooked through and slightly charred, about 20-25 minutes, turning occasionally to ensure even cooking.
5. While the chicken is grilling or roasting, prepare the coconut gravy. In a small saucepan, combine the coconut milk, tamarind paste, water, brown sugar, and salt. Stir to combine.
6. Bring the coconut gravy to a gentle simmer over medium heat. Let it cook for about 5-7 minutes, stirring occasionally, until slightly thickened.
7. Once the chicken is cooked, remove it from the grill or oven and transfer it to a serving platter.
8. Pour the coconut gravy over the grilled or roasted chicken pieces.
9. Serve the Ayam Percik hot with steamed rice or as part of a Malay feast.
10. Enjoy your delicious and flavorful Ayam Percik! Adjust the spice level according to your preference by adding more or fewer dried red chilies to the spice paste.

Curry Laksa

Ingredients:

For the Laksa Paste:

- 6 dried red chilies, soaked in hot water for 15 minutes
- 4 shallots, peeled
- 3 cloves garlic, peeled
- 1-inch piece ginger, peeled
- 1-inch piece galangal, peeled
- 2 stalks lemongrass, white part only, thinly sliced
- 1 tablespoon ground coriander
- 1 teaspoon ground turmeric
- 1 teaspoon ground cumin
- 1 tablespoon shrimp paste (belacan)
- 2 tablespoons vegetable oil

For the Soup:

- 4 cups chicken or vegetable broth
- 2 cups coconut milk
- 2 kaffir lime leaves
- 1 tablespoon brown sugar or palm sugar
- 1 tablespoon fish sauce
- Salt to taste

For the Toppings (optional):

- Cooked chicken, shrimp, tofu puffs, fish cakes, or any other protein of your choice
- Cooked egg noodles or rice vermicelli, soaked in hot water until softened
- Bean sprouts
- Hard-boiled eggs, halved
- Chopped cilantro and lime wedges for garnish

Instructions:

1. To make the Laksa paste, drain the soaked dried red chilies and place them in a blender or food processor. Add the shallots, garlic, ginger, galangal, sliced lemongrass, ground coriander, ground turmeric, ground cumin, and shrimp paste. Blend until you get a smooth paste.
2. Heat the vegetable oil in a large pot over medium heat. Add the Laksa paste to the pot and cook, stirring constantly, for about 5-7 minutes until fragrant.
3. Pour in the chicken or vegetable broth and coconut milk. Add the kaffir lime leaves, brown sugar or palm sugar, and fish sauce. Stir to combine.
4. Bring the Laksa soup to a gentle simmer and let it cook for about 10-15 minutes to allow the flavors to meld together. Taste and adjust the seasoning with salt if needed.
5. While the soup is simmering, prepare your desired toppings by cooking the protein of your choice and any vegetables you'd like to add.
6. To serve, divide the cooked egg noodles or rice vermicelli among serving bowls. Ladle the hot Laksa soup over the noodles.
7. Arrange the cooked protein, tofu puffs, bean sprouts, and halved hard-boiled eggs on top of the noodles.
8. Garnish the Curry Laksa with chopped cilantro and serve with lime wedges on the side.
9. Enjoy your delicious and aromatic Curry Laksa! Adjust the spiciness level by adding more or fewer dried red chilies to the Laksa paste according to your preference.

Nasi Goreng

Ingredients:

- 3 cups cooked white rice, preferably cooled or leftover
- 2 tablespoons vegetable oil
- 2 cloves garlic, minced
- 1 small onion, finely chopped
- 2 eggs, lightly beaten
- 1 cup cooked chicken, shrimp, or tofu (optional)
- 1 cup mixed vegetables (such as peas, carrots, and bell peppers)
- 2 tablespoons sweet soy sauce (kecap manis)
- 1 tablespoon soy sauce
- 1 teaspoon shrimp paste (terasi), optional
- Salt and pepper to taste
- Sliced cucumber and tomato, for garnish
- Fried shallots or scallions, for garnish
- Lime wedges, for serving

Instructions:

1. Heat the vegetable oil in a large wok or skillet over medium heat. Add the minced garlic and chopped onion, and cook until softened and fragrant, about 2-3 minutes.
2. Push the garlic and onion to one side of the wok and pour the beaten eggs into the empty space. Scramble the eggs until cooked through, then mix them with the garlic and onion.
3. Add the cooked chicken, shrimp, or tofu (if using) to the wok, along with the mixed vegetables. Stir-fry for a few minutes until the vegetables are tender.
4. Add the cooked white rice to the wok, breaking up any clumps with a spatula. Stir-fry the rice with the other ingredients for a few minutes until heated through.
5. Drizzle the sweet soy sauce and soy sauce over the rice. If using shrimp paste, add it now. Stir well to combine all the ingredients evenly.
6. Season the Nasi Goreng with salt and pepper to taste. Be cautious with the salt if your soy sauce is already salty.
7. Continue to stir-fry the Nasi Goreng for another 2-3 minutes until everything is well mixed and heated through.
8. Transfer the Nasi Goreng to serving plates or bowls. Garnish with sliced cucumber, tomato, fried shallots or scallions, and lime wedges.
9. Serve the Nasi Goreng hot, with additional soy sauce or chili sauce on the side if desired.
10. Enjoy your delicious Indonesian-style fried rice! Nasi Goreng is versatile, so feel free to customize it with your favorite proteins and vegetables.

Nasi Kerabu

Ingredients:

For the Blue Rice:

- 2 cups jasmine rice
- 2 cups water
- 1 cup coconut milk
- 1 tablespoon dried butterfly pea flowers

For the Kerabu Salad:

- 1 cup finely shredded cabbage
- 1 cup bean sprouts
- 1 cup finely sliced long beans, blanched
- 1 cup grated coconut, toasted
- 1 cup fresh herbs (mint leaves, Vietnamese coriander, basil), chopped
- 1 cup cucumber, julienned
- 1 cup carrots, julienned
- 1 cup fried shallots

For the Protein (choose one or more):

- Grilled chicken, sliced
- Fried fish, flaked
- Boiled shrimp
- Fried tofu or tempeh, sliced

For the Sambal (Spicy Sauce):

- 5-6 dried red chilies, soaked in hot water
- 3 shallots, peeled
- 2 cloves garlic, peeled
- 1 tablespoon dried shrimp, soaked in hot water (optional)
- 1 tablespoon tamarind paste, dissolved in 2 tablespoons warm water
- 1 tablespoon brown sugar
- Salt to taste

Instructions:

1. Rinse the jasmine rice under cold water until the water runs clear. Drain well.
2. In a rice cooker or pot, combine the rice, water, coconut milk, and dried butterfly pea flowers. Cook the rice according to your rice cooker's instructions or until fluffy and cooked through.
3. While the rice is cooking, prepare the Kerabu salad. In a large mixing bowl, combine the shredded cabbage, bean sprouts, blanched long beans, toasted grated coconut, chopped fresh herbs, julienned cucumber, julienned carrots, and fried shallots. Toss everything together until well mixed. Set aside.
4. Prepare the protein of your choice (grilled chicken, fried fish, boiled shrimp, or fried tofu/tempeh) according to your preference. Set aside.
5. To make the sambal, drain the soaked dried red chilies and place them in a blender or food processor. Add the peeled shallots, peeled garlic, and soaked dried shrimp (if using). Blend until you get a smooth paste.
6. Transfer the chili paste to a small saucepan. Add the tamarind paste mixture, brown sugar, and salt to taste. Cook the sambal over medium heat for about 5-7 minutes, stirring occasionally, until it thickens slightly. Remove from heat and set aside.
7. Once the rice is cooked, remove the dried butterfly pea flowers and fluff the rice with a fork.
8. To assemble the Nasi Kerabu, place a portion of the blue rice on a serving plate. Arrange a generous amount of the Kerabu salad and your chosen protein(s) on top of the rice.
9. Serve the Nasi Kerabu with a side of the prepared sambal.
10. Enjoy your vibrant and flavorful Nasi Kerabu! Adjust the ingredients and toppings according to your taste preferences.

Sambal Udang (Spicy Chili Shrimp)

Ingredients:

- 1 lb (about 450g) large shrimp, peeled and deveined
- 2 tablespoons vegetable oil
- 3 cloves garlic, minced
- 1 small onion, finely chopped
- 3-4 red chili peppers, finely chopped (adjust according to spice preference)
- 2 tablespoons tomato paste
- 1 tablespoon tamarind paste, dissolved in 2 tablespoons warm water
- 1 tablespoon brown sugar
- Salt to taste
- Lime wedges and chopped cilantro, for garnish

Instructions:

1. Heat the vegetable oil in a large skillet or wok over medium-high heat.
2. Add the minced garlic and chopped onion to the skillet. Stir-fry for 1-2 minutes until fragrant and the onion is translucent.
3. Add the chopped red chili peppers to the skillet. Stir-fry for another 1-2 minutes until the chili peppers begin to soften.
4. Stir in the tomato paste and cook for 1-2 minutes until fragrant and well combined with the other ingredients.
5. Add the peeled and deveined shrimp to the skillet. Stir-fry for 2-3 minutes until the shrimp turn pink and opaque.
6. Pour in the dissolved tamarind paste (tamarind water), brown sugar, and salt to taste. Stir well to coat the shrimp evenly with the sauce.
7. Cook for another 2-3 minutes, stirring occasionally, until the sauce thickens slightly and coats the shrimp.
8. Once the shrimp is cooked through and the sauce has thickened to your desired consistency, remove the skillet from heat.
9. Transfer the Sambal Udang to a serving dish.
10. Garnish with lime wedges and chopped cilantro.
11. Serve hot with steamed rice or as part of a Malaysian meal.
12. Enjoy your spicy and flavorful Sambal Udang! Adjust the amount of chili peppers according to your spice preference.

Assam Pedas

Ingredients:

- 1 lb (about 450g) fish fillets (such as mackerel), cut into chunks
- 2 tablespoons vegetable oil
- 3 cloves garlic, minced
- 1 small onion, thinly sliced
- 2-3 red chili peppers, sliced (adjust to taste)
- 1 tablespoon tamarind paste, dissolved in 1 cup warm water
- 2 tablespoons fish sauce
- 1 tablespoon palm sugar or brown sugar
- Salt to taste
- Assorted vegetables (such as tomatoes, okra, eggplant, and long beans), chopped
- Fresh cilantro, chopped, for garnish

Instructions:

1. Heat the vegetable oil in a large skillet or wok over medium heat.
2. Add the minced garlic and sliced onion to the skillet. Stir-fry for 1-2 minutes until fragrant and the onion is softened.
3. Add the sliced red chili peppers to the skillet. Stir-fry for another 1-2 minutes.
4. Pour in the tamarind water (dissolved tamarind paste), fish sauce, and palm sugar (or brown sugar). Stir well to combine.
5. Bring the mixture to a simmer and let it cook for 5-7 minutes, allowing the flavors to meld together and the sauce to thicken slightly.
6. Taste the sauce and adjust the seasoning with salt if needed.
7. Add the chopped vegetables to the skillet. Stir to coat them with the sauce.
8. Gently add the fish fillets to the skillet, making sure they are submerged in the sauce.
9. Cover the skillet and let the Assam Pedas simmer for 8-10 minutes, or until the fish is cooked through and the vegetables are tender.
10. Once the fish is cooked, remove the skillet from heat.
11. Transfer the Assam Pedas to a serving dish.
12. Garnish with fresh chopped cilantro.
13. Serve hot with steamed rice.
14. Enjoy your tangy and spicy Assam Pedas! Adjust the level of spiciness and sourness according to your taste preferences.

Murtabak

Ingredients:

For the Pancake Dough:

- 2 cups all-purpose flour
- 1/2 teaspoon salt
- 1 tablespoon vegetable oil
- 3/4 cup water

For the Filling:

- 1 lb (about 450g) minced meat (chicken, beef, or lamb)
- 1 onion, finely chopped
- 2 cloves garlic, minced
- 1 teaspoon ground cumin
- 1 teaspoon ground coriander
- 1/2 teaspoon ground turmeric
- Salt and pepper to taste
- Vegetable oil for frying

For Serving (optional):

- Cucumber slices
- Tomato slices
- Onion slices
- Cilantro leaves
- Pickled onions
- Curry sauce or curry gravy

Instructions:

1. In a large mixing bowl, combine the all-purpose flour and salt. Gradually add the water while stirring, until a smooth dough forms. Knead the dough for about 5 minutes until it becomes elastic. Cover with a damp cloth and let it rest for 30 minutes.

2. While the dough is resting, prepare the filling. In a skillet, heat some vegetable oil over medium heat. Add the minced meat, chopped onion, and minced garlic. Cook until the meat is browned and the onions are soft.
3. Add the ground cumin, ground coriander, ground turmeric, salt, and pepper to the skillet. Stir well to combine. Cook for another 2-3 minutes to allow the flavors to meld together. Remove from heat and set aside.
4. Divide the dough into equal-sized balls. On a lightly floured surface, roll out each dough ball into a thin circle, about 8-10 inches in diameter.
5. Place a generous amount of the meat filling onto one half of the dough circle, leaving a border around the edges.
6. Fold the other half of the dough circle over the filling to create a half-moon shape. Press the edges firmly to seal.
7. Heat some vegetable oil in a large skillet or griddle over medium heat. Carefully transfer the stuffed dough to the skillet and cook for about 3-4 minutes on each side, or until golden brown and crispy.
8. Once cooked, remove the murtabak from the skillet and drain on paper towels to remove excess oil.
9. Slice the murtabak into wedges and serve hot with cucumber slices, tomato slices, onion slices, cilantro leaves, pickled onions, and curry sauce or curry gravy on the side.
10. Enjoy your delicious homemade murtabak as a snack or meal!

Nasi Ayam (Chicken Rice)

Ingredients:

For the Chicken:

- 1 whole chicken (about 3-4 lbs)
- 2 stalks lemongrass, smashed
- 4 slices ginger
- 4 cloves garlic, smashed
- 2 tablespoons soy sauce
- Salt to taste

For the Rice:

- 2 cups jasmine rice, washed and drained
- 2 cups chicken broth (or water)
- 2 slices ginger
- 2 cloves garlic, smashed
- 2 pandan leaves (optional)
- Salt to taste

For the Chili Sauce:

- 5-6 red chili peppers, seeded and chopped
- 2 cloves garlic
- 1 inch ginger
- 1 tablespoon lime juice
- 1 tablespoon soy sauce
- 1 tablespoon sugar
- Salt to taste

For the Ginger Garlic Sauce:

- 4 cloves garlic
- 1 inch ginger
- 2 tablespoons chicken broth
- 1 tablespoon soy sauce

- 1 tablespoon sesame oil
- Salt to taste

For Garnish:

- Cucumber slices
- Tomato slices
- Fresh cilantro or parsley

Instructions:

1. Prepare the chicken by rinsing it under cold water and patting it dry with paper towels. Rub the chicken with salt inside and out.
2. In a large pot, bring water to a boil. Add the smashed lemongrass, ginger slices, smashed garlic cloves, and soy sauce. Place the whole chicken into the pot, breast side down. Add enough water to cover the chicken. Bring it to a boil, then reduce the heat to low and simmer for about 40-50 minutes, or until the chicken is cooked through.
3. While the chicken is cooking, prepare the rice. In a rice cooker or pot, combine the washed and drained jasmine rice with chicken broth (or water), ginger slices, smashed garlic cloves, pandan leaves (if using), and salt to taste. Cook the rice according to your rice cooker's instructions or until fluffy and cooked through.
4. While the chicken and rice are cooking, prepare the chili sauce and ginger garlic sauce. For the chili sauce, blend the chopped red chili peppers, garlic, ginger, lime juice, soy sauce, sugar, and salt until smooth. For the ginger garlic sauce, blend the garlic, ginger, chicken broth, soy sauce, sesame oil, and salt until smooth.
5. Once the chicken is cooked, remove it from the pot and plunge it into a bowl of ice water for a few minutes to stop the cooking process and keep the skin firm.
6. After the chicken has cooled, remove it from the ice water and pat it dry with paper towels. Rub the chicken with a little sesame oil for extra flavor and shine.
7. Slice the chicken into serving pieces.
8. To serve, plate a portion of the fragrant rice onto each serving plate. Arrange slices of chicken on top of the rice. Serve with cucumber slices, tomato slices, fresh cilantro or parsley, and the chili sauce and ginger garlic sauce on the side.
9. Enjoy your delicious Nasi Ayam! Adjust the sauces according to your taste preferences.

Apam Balik (Malaysian Pancake)

Ingredients:

For the Batter:

- 1 cup all-purpose flour
- 1/4 cup rice flour
- 1/4 teaspoon baking powder
- 1/4 teaspoon baking soda
- 1/4 teaspoon salt
- 2 tablespoons granulated sugar
- 1 egg
- 1 cup coconut milk
- 1/4 cup water

For the Filling (optional):

- Crushed roasted peanuts
- Granulated sugar
- Creamed corn
- Butter or margarine

Instructions:

1. In a large mixing bowl, combine the all-purpose flour, rice flour, baking powder, baking soda, salt, and granulated sugar.
2. In a separate bowl, whisk together the egg, coconut milk, and water until well combined.
3. Gradually pour the wet ingredients into the dry ingredients while whisking continuously until you get a smooth batter. Let the batter rest for about 30 minutes to allow the flavors to meld together.
4. Heat a non-stick skillet or pan over medium heat. Lightly grease the surface with a little oil or butter.
5. Pour a ladleful of the batter onto the skillet and spread it out into a thin circle, about 6-8 inches in diameter.
6. Cook the pancake for 2-3 minutes, or until bubbles start to form on the surface and the edges begin to lift.
7. Once the bottom is golden brown and crispy, flip the pancake over using a spatula.
8. Spread a thin layer of butter or margarine on the cooked side of the pancake (optional).

9. Sprinkle crushed roasted peanuts, granulated sugar, and creamed corn over half of the pancake.
10. Fold the pancake in half to enclose the filling, forming a half-moon shape.
11. Continue to cook the pancake for another 1-2 minutes, or until the filling is heated through and the pancake is crispy and golden brown on both sides.
12. Remove the pancake from the skillet and transfer it to a plate.
13. Repeat the process with the remaining batter and filling ingredients.
14. Serve the Apam Balik warm as a delicious snack or dessert.
15. Enjoy your homemade Malaysian Pancake! Feel free to customize the filling according to your preferences.

Lontong

Ingredients:

For the Lontong:

- 2 cups rice, washed and soaked for 3-4 hours
- Banana leaves, cleaned and cut into squares (about 8x8 inches)

For the Peanut Sauce:

- 1 cup unsalted peanuts, roasted and finely ground
- 2 cloves garlic, minced
- 2 shallots, minced
- 2-3 red chili peppers, finely chopped
- 1 tablespoon tamarind paste, dissolved in 1/4 cup warm water
- 2 tablespoons palm sugar or brown sugar
- Salt to taste
- Water as needed

For Serving (optional):

- Sambal (chili paste)
- Sliced cucumber
- Fried tofu or tempeh
- Hard-boiled eggs, halved
- Fried anchovies
- Fried shallots
- Fresh cilantro or parsley

Instructions:

1. Drain the soaked rice and grind it into a smooth paste using a food processor or blender. Add a little water if needed to help with blending.
2. Place a few spoonfuls of the rice paste onto the center of each banana leaf square. Fold and roll the banana leaf to enclose the rice, then secure the edges by folding them and tying with kitchen twine. Repeat until all the rice paste is used up.

3. Place the wrapped rice cakes (Lontong) in a large pot of boiling water. Cook for about 2-3 hours until the rice cakes are firm and cooked through. Remove from the water and let them cool slightly before unwrapping.
4. While the Lontong is cooking, prepare the peanut sauce. In a saucepan, heat a little oil over medium heat. Add the minced garlic, shallots, and chopped chili peppers. Cook until fragrant and the shallots are softened.
5. Add the ground peanuts to the saucepan and stir well to combine with the aromatics.
6. Pour in the tamarind water, palm sugar or brown sugar, and salt to taste. Stir continuously and let the sauce simmer gently for about 5-10 minutes until thickened. Add more water if needed to achieve the desired consistency.
7. Once the peanut sauce is ready, remove it from the heat and let it cool slightly.
8. To serve, unwrap the Lontong from the banana leaves and cut them into thick slices.
9. Arrange the Lontong slices on serving plates and drizzle generously with the peanut sauce.
10. Serve with additional side dishes such as sambal, sliced cucumber, fried tofu or tempeh, hard-boiled eggs, fried anchovies, fried shallots, and fresh cilantro or parsley.
11. Enjoy your delicious Lontong with Peanut Sauce, a traditional Indonesian and Malaysian delicacy! Adjust the spiciness and sweetness of the peanut sauce according to your taste preferences.

Mee Rebus

Ingredients:

For the Gravy:

- 1 sweet potato, peeled and cubed
- 2 cloves garlic, minced
- 1-inch piece ginger, minced
- 2 tablespoons dried shrimp, soaked in hot water (optional)
- 2 tablespoons dried anchovies (ikan bilis), soaked in hot water (optional)
- 1 tablespoon ground coriander
- 1 tablespoon ground turmeric
- 1 teaspoon ground cumin
- 1 teaspoon chili powder (adjust to taste)
- 4 cups water or chicken stock
- 1 cup coconut milk
- 2 tablespoons tamarind paste, dissolved in 1/4 cup warm water
- 2 tablespoons palm sugar or brown sugar
- Salt to taste

For Serving:

- Yellow noodles, blanched
- Hard-boiled eggs, halved
- Fried tofu, sliced
- Bean sprouts, blanched
- Fresh cilantro or parsley, chopped
- Fried shallots

Instructions:

1. In a blender or food processor, combine the sweet potato, garlic, ginger, soaked dried shrimp (if using), soaked dried anchovies (if using), ground coriander, ground turmeric, ground cumin, and chili powder. Blend until you get a smooth paste, adding a little water if needed.
2. Heat a little oil in a large pot over medium heat. Add the blended paste and cook for 2-3 minutes until fragrant.
3. Pour in the water or chicken stock, coconut milk, and dissolved tamarind paste. Stir well to combine.

4. Bring the gravy to a boil, then reduce the heat to low and let it simmer for about 15-20 minutes, stirring occasionally, until the sweet potato is cooked through and the gravy has thickened.
5. Add the palm sugar or brown sugar to the gravy and stir until dissolved. Season with salt to taste.
6. While the gravy is simmering, prepare the toppings by blanching the yellow noodles, bean sprouts, and frying the tofu.
7. To serve, place a portion of blanched yellow noodles in a serving bowl. Ladle the hot gravy over the noodles.
8. Garnish with hard-boiled eggs, fried tofu slices, blanched bean sprouts, chopped fresh cilantro or parsley, and fried shallots.
9. Serve the Mee Rebus hot and enjoy!

Feel free to customize the toppings according to your preference. Some common additional toppings include sliced green chilies, lime wedges, and fried onions. Adjust the spiciness and sweetness of the gravy according to your taste preference.

Kuih Ketayap (Pandan Crepes)

Ingredients:

For the Crepes:

- 1 cup all-purpose flour
- 1/4 cup rice flour
- 1/4 teaspoon salt
- 2 eggs
- 1 cup coconut milk
- 1/2 cup pandan juice (made from blending 8-10 pandan leaves with water and straining)
- Green food coloring (optional)
- Vegetable oil for cooking

For the Filling:

- 1 cup grated coconut (fresh or desiccated)
- 1/2 cup palm sugar or brown sugar
- 1/4 cup water
- 1 pandan leaf, knotted

Instructions:

1. In a mixing bowl, combine the all-purpose flour, rice flour, and salt.
2. In a separate bowl, whisk together the eggs, coconut milk, pandan juice, and green food coloring (if using) until well combined.
3. Gradually pour the wet ingredients into the dry ingredients, whisking continuously until you get a smooth batter. Let the batter rest for about 30 minutes to allow the flavors to meld together.
4. While the batter is resting, prepare the coconut filling. In a saucepan, combine the grated coconut, palm sugar or brown sugar, water, and knotted pandan leaf. Cook over medium heat, stirring constantly, until the sugar has dissolved and the mixture is slightly thickened. Remove from heat and let it cool.
5. Heat a non-stick skillet or crepe pan over medium heat. Lightly grease the surface with a little oil.
6. Pour a ladleful of the batter onto the skillet and swirl it around to coat the bottom evenly, forming a thin crepe. Cook for about 1-2 minutes until the edges start to lift and the bottom is lightly browned.

7. Flip the crepe over and cook for another 1-2 minutes until cooked through and lightly browned. Remove from the skillet and set aside. Repeat with the remaining batter.
8. To assemble the Kuih Ketayap, place a spoonful of the coconut filling onto one end of each crepe. Fold the sides over the filling and roll it up tightly to form a cylinder. Repeat with the remaining crepes and filling.
9. Serve the Kuih Ketayap warm or at room temperature as a delightful snack or dessert.
10. Enjoy your homemade Kuih Ketayap, filled with delicious sweet coconut goodness! Adjust the sweetness of the filling according to your taste preference.

Penang Hokkien Mee

Ingredients:

For the Soup Base:

- 1 lb (about 450g) prawns, shells removed and reserved, heads removed and deveined
- 1 lb (about 450g) pork bones or chicken bones
- 6 cups water
- 1 large onion, peeled and halved
- 4 cloves garlic, smashed
- 2-inch piece ginger, sliced
- 2 tablespoons dried shrimp, soaked in hot water for 15 minutes
- 2 tablespoons dried anchovies (ikan bilis), soaked in hot water for 15 minutes
- 2 tablespoons ground dried shrimp paste (belacan)
- 2 tablespoons vegetable oil
- 2 tablespoons soy sauce
- Salt to taste

For the Noodles and Toppings:

- 1 lb (about 450g) yellow noodles
- 1/2 lb (about 225g) rice vermicelli (bihun)
- 1 cup bean sprouts, blanched
- Hard-boiled eggs, halved
- Fresh cilantro or parsley, chopped
- Fried shallots

For the Chili Paste (Sambal):

- 10-12 dried red chilies, seeded and soaked in hot water for 15 minutes
- 3 cloves garlic
- 2 shallots
- 1 tablespoon shrimp paste (belacan)
- 1 tablespoon vegetable oil
- Salt to taste

Instructions:

1. To prepare the soup base, heat the vegetable oil in a large pot over medium heat. Add the reserved prawn shells and heads, pork bones or chicken bones, onion, garlic, and ginger. Cook until the ingredients are fragrant and lightly browned.
2. Add the soaked dried shrimp, soaked dried anchovies, and ground dried shrimp paste (belacan) to the pot. Stir well to combine.
3. Pour in the water and bring the mixture to a boil. Reduce the heat to low and let it simmer for about 1-2 hours, uncovered, to allow the flavors to develop and the broth to reduce.
4. Once the broth has simmered and reduced, strain it through a fine mesh sieve into another pot. Discard the solids and return the strained broth to the stove.
5. Bring the broth back to a simmer and season with soy sauce and salt to taste. Keep the broth warm while you prepare the noodles and toppings.
6. To make the chili paste (sambal), blend the soaked dried red chilies, garlic, shallots, and shrimp paste (belacan) until smooth. Heat the vegetable oil in a small skillet or saucepan over medium heat. Add the blended chili paste and cook for 5-7 minutes, stirring constantly, until fragrant and the oil separates. Season with salt to taste and set aside.
7. Cook the yellow noodles and rice vermicelli in a pot of boiling water according to the package instructions. Drain and set aside.
8. To serve, divide the cooked noodles and bean sprouts among serving bowls. Ladle the hot soup broth over the noodles.
9. Top each bowl with cooked prawns, hard-boiled eggs, chopped cilantro or parsley, and fried shallots.
10. Serve the Penang Hokkien Mee hot with the chili paste (sambal) on the side for extra spiciness. Enjoy your delicious and flavorful noodle soup!

Adjust the spiciness of the chili paste according to your taste preference. You can also customize the toppings with additional ingredients such as sliced chicken, squid, or fish cake.

Kari Ayam (Chicken Curry)

Ingredients:

For the Curry Paste:

- 3 shallots, chopped
- 4 cloves garlic, chopped
- 1-inch piece ginger, chopped
- 2 stalks lemongrass, white parts only, chopped
- 2 red chili peppers, chopped (adjust to taste)
- 1 tablespoon ground coriander
- 1 teaspoon ground cumin
- 1/2 teaspoon ground turmeric
- 1/2 teaspoon chili powder (optional, for extra heat)
- 2 tablespoons vegetable oil

For the Chicken Curry:

- 1 whole chicken, cut into pieces (or use chicken thighs or drumsticks)
- 2 potatoes, peeled and cut into cubes
- 1 onion, sliced
- 1 cup coconut milk
- 2 cups chicken broth or water
- 2 tablespoons tamarind paste, dissolved in 1/4 cup warm water
- Salt to taste
- Sugar to taste (optional)
- Fresh cilantro or parsley, chopped, for garnish

Instructions:

1. In a blender or food processor, combine all the ingredients for the curry paste. Blend until you get a smooth paste.
2. Heat the vegetable oil in a large pot or Dutch oven over medium heat. Add the curry paste and cook, stirring constantly, for 2-3 minutes until fragrant.
3. Add the sliced onions to the pot and cook for another 2-3 minutes until softened.
4. Add the chicken pieces to the pot and stir to coat them evenly with the curry paste.
5. Pour in the chicken broth or water and bring the mixture to a simmer. Cover the pot and let it cook for about 20-25 minutes until the chicken is almost cooked through.

6. Add the cubed potatoes to the pot and continue to simmer, covered, for another 10-15 minutes until the potatoes are tender and the chicken is fully cooked.
7. Stir in the coconut milk and tamarind water mixture. Season with salt to taste. Add sugar if desired for a slightly sweeter flavor.
8. Let the curry simmer for another 5-10 minutes to allow the flavors to meld together and the sauce to thicken slightly.
9. Once the chicken curry is ready, remove it from the heat.
10. Serve the Kari Ayam hot, garnished with chopped cilantro or parsley.
11. Enjoy your delicious Chicken Curry with steamed rice or bread of your choice!

Feel free to adjust the spiciness of the curry by adding more or fewer chili peppers according to your taste preference. You can also add other vegetables such as carrots or bell peppers if desired.

Nasi Dagang

Ingredients:

For the Rice:

- 2 cups glutinous rice
- 1 cup jasmine rice
- 4 cups water
- 1 cup coconut milk
- 1 teaspoon salt

For the Fish Curry:

- 500g mackerel or tuna fillets, cut into chunks
- 1 onion, sliced
- 2 cloves garlic, minced
- 1-inch piece ginger, minced
- 2 stalks lemongrass, smashed
- 2 tablespoons fish curry powder
- 1 cup coconut milk
- 2 cups water
- Salt to taste
- Vegetable oil for cooking

For the Side Dishes:

- Hard-boiled eggs, halved
- Sliced cucumber
- Sambal (chili paste)
- Fried anchovies (ikan bilis)
- Fried shallots
- Fresh herbs (such as cilantro or parsley)

Instructions:

1. Rinse the glutinous rice and jasmine rice under cold water until the water runs clear. Drain well.
2. In a rice cooker or pot, combine the rice, water, coconut milk, and salt. Cook the rice according to your rice cooker's instructions or until it's fluffy and cooked through.
3. While the rice is cooking, prepare the fish curry. Heat some vegetable oil in a large pot or skillet over medium heat.
4. Add the sliced onion, minced garlic, minced ginger, and smashed lemongrass to the pot. Cook until the onions are softened and aromatic.
5. Stir in the fish curry powder and cook for another 1-2 minutes until fragrant.
6. Add the fish fillets to the pot and cook for a few minutes until they start to turn opaque.
7. Pour in the coconut milk and water. Bring the mixture to a simmer and let it cook for about 10-15 minutes until the fish is cooked through and the curry has thickened slightly. Season with salt to taste.
8. Once the rice and fish curry are ready, serve the Nasi Dagang hot with the side dishes.
9. To serve, place a portion of the steamed rice on a plate or banana leaf. Ladle the fish curry over the rice.
10. Garnish with hard-boiled eggs, sliced cucumber, sambal, fried anchovies, fried shallots, and fresh herbs.
11. Enjoy your delicious Nasi Dagang, a traditional Malaysian delicacy! Adjust the spiciness of the curry according to your taste preference.

Rojak

Ingredients:

For the Salad:

- 1 large cucumber, peeled and sliced
- 1 small jicama (yam bean), peeled and julienned
- 1 small pineapple, peeled and cut into chunks
- 1 small green apple, julienned
- 1 small firm tofu, cut into cubes and fried (optional)
- 1 small cucumber, peeled and cut into cubes (optional)
- 1 small unripe mango, julienned (optional)
- 1 small guava, sliced (optional)
- 1 small rose apple, sliced (optional)
- 1 small papaya, sliced (optional)
- 1 small starfruit, sliced (optional)
- 1 small handful of roasted peanuts, coarsely chopped
- 1 small handful of fried shallots

For the Dressing:

- 4 tablespoons palm sugar or brown sugar
- 3 tablespoons tamarind paste, dissolved in 1/4 cup warm water
- 2 tablespoons shrimp paste (belacan), roasted
- 2 tablespoons soy sauce
- 2 tablespoons lime juice
- 1-2 red chili peppers, seeded and chopped (adjust to taste)
- 1 garlic clove, minced
- Salt to taste

Instructions:

1. In a large mixing bowl, combine all the fruits and vegetables for the salad. Toss well to mix.
2. In a separate bowl, prepare the dressing by combining the palm sugar, dissolved tamarind paste, roasted shrimp paste, soy sauce, lime juice, chopped red chili peppers, minced garlic, and salt. Stir until the sugar has dissolved and the ingredients are well combined.
3. Pour the dressing over the salad and toss gently to coat all the ingredients evenly.

4. Transfer the salad to a serving platter or individual plates.
5. Sprinkle the chopped roasted peanuts and fried shallots over the salad as a garnish.
6. Serve the Rojak immediately as a refreshing and flavorful appetizer or snack.
7. Enjoy your delicious Rojak, packed with a delightful mix of flavors and textures!

Feel free to adjust the ingredients and dressing according to your taste preference. You can add or omit fruits and vegetables based on availability and personal preference.

Acar

Ingredients:

For the Pickling Solution:

- 1 cup white vinegar
- 1 cup water
- 1/2 cup sugar
- 1 teaspoon salt

For the Vegetables:

- 1 cucumber, julienned
- 2 carrots, julienned
- 1 small cabbage, thinly sliced
- 2 shallots, thinly sliced
- 2-3 red chili peppers, thinly sliced
- 2 cloves garlic, minced

For the Spice Paste:

- 4-5 dried red chili peppers, soaked in hot water for 15 minutes
- 2 cloves garlic
- 1-inch piece ginger
- 1 teaspoon ground turmeric
- 1 teaspoon ground coriander
- 1 teaspoon ground cumin
- 1 tablespoon vegetable oil

Instructions:

1. Prepare the pickling solution by combining white vinegar, water, sugar, and salt in a saucepan. Heat the mixture over medium heat, stirring occasionally, until the sugar and salt are fully dissolved. Remove from heat and let it cool completely.
2. Meanwhile, prepare the vegetables by julienned cucumber and carrots, thinly slicing the cabbage and shallots, and thinly slicing the red chili peppers. Place all the vegetables in a large mixing bowl.

3. Make the spice paste by blending soaked dried red chili peppers, garlic, ginger, ground turmeric, ground coriander, and ground cumin in a food processor or blender until smooth.
4. Heat vegetable oil in a skillet over medium heat. Add the spice paste and minced garlic, and sauté for 2-3 minutes until fragrant.
5. Pour the cooled pickling solution over the vegetables in the mixing bowl. Add the sautéed spice paste and garlic to the vegetables. Toss well to coat all the vegetables evenly.
6. Transfer the acar mixture to a clean and sterilized glass jar or container.
7. Seal the jar or container tightly and let it marinate in the refrigerator for at least 24 hours before serving, to allow the flavors to develop.
8. Serve the acar as a tangy and spicy condiment alongside rice dishes, grilled meats, or as a refreshing side dish.
9. Enjoy your homemade acar, packed with vibrant flavors and crunchy textures!

Feel free to adjust the spiciness and sweetness of the acar by adding more or less chili peppers and sugar according to your taste preference.

Mee Siam

- 2 tablespoons vegetable oil

For the Gravy:

- 2 tablespoons tamarind pulp, soaked in 1/2 cup warm water, then strained to obtain tamarind juice
- 3 tablespoons vegetable oil
- 2 cloves garlic, minced
- 1 small onion, finely chopped
- 2 tablespoons dried shrimp, soaked in hot water for 15 minutes, then drained and finely chopped
- 2 tablespoons chili paste or sambal oelek (adjust to taste)
- 1 tablespoon tomato paste
- 1 tablespoon palm sugar or brown sugar
- 1 teaspoon ground coriander
- 1 teaspoon ground cumin
- 1/2 teaspoon turmeric powder
- 1/2 cup coconut milk
- Salt to taste

For Toppings (Optional):

- Hard-boiled eggs, halved
- Bean sprouts
- Fried tofu cubes
- Fried shallots
- Fresh cilantro or parsley, chopped
- Lime wedges

Instructions:

1. Heat 2 tablespoons of vegetable oil in a large skillet or wok over medium heat. Add the drained rice vermicelli noodles and stir-fry for 2-3 minutes until heated through and lightly browned. Remove from the skillet and set aside.
2. In the same skillet or wok, heat 3 tablespoons of vegetable oil over medium heat. Add the minced garlic and chopped onion, and cook until softened and fragrant.
3. Add the chopped dried shrimp to the skillet and cook for 1-2 minutes until aromatic.

4. Stir in the chili paste or sambal oelek, tomato paste, palm sugar or brown sugar, ground coriander, ground cumin, and turmeric powder. Cook for another 2-3 minutes until the spices are fragrant and well combined.
5. Pour in the tamarind juice and coconut milk, and bring the mixture to a simmer. Let it cook for 5-7 minutes until the gravy has thickened slightly.
6. Season the gravy with salt to taste.
7. To serve, place a portion of the stir-fried rice vermicelli noodles on a plate. Ladle the hot gravy over the noodles.
8. Garnish with your choice of toppings such as halved hard-boiled eggs, bean sprouts, fried tofu cubes, fried shallots, chopped cilantro or parsley, and lime wedges.
9. Serve the Mee Siam hot and enjoy the delicious combination of flavors!

Feel free to adjust the spiciness and sweetness of the gravy according to your taste preference.

You can also add other toppings such as shrimp, chicken, or sliced fish cakes if desired.

Prawn Mee

Ingredients:

For the Broth:

- 500g prawns, shells and heads removed (reserve the meat for garnish)
- 1 onion, peeled and halved
- 4 cloves garlic, smashed
- 2-inch piece ginger, sliced
- 2 stalks lemongrass, white parts only, smashed
- 2 tablespoons vegetable oil
- 1 tablespoon shrimp paste (belacan)
- 1 tablespoon ground coriander
- 1 teaspoon ground turmeric
- 1 teaspoon ground white pepper
- 6 cups water
- Salt to taste

For the Noodles:

- 400g yellow noodles
- 400g rice vermicelli noodles (bihun)
- Bean sprouts, blanched
- Hard-boiled eggs, halved
- Cooked prawns (reserved from the broth)
- Chopped scallions (spring onions)
- Chopped cilantro (coriander)
- Sambal chili paste (optional)
- Lime wedges

Instructions:

1. Peel and devein the prawns, reserving the shells and heads. Set aside the prawn meat for garnish.
2. In a large pot, heat the vegetable oil over medium heat. Add the prawn shells and heads, onion, garlic, ginger, and lemongrass. Cook, stirring occasionally, until the shells turn pink and aromatic.

3. Stir in the shrimp paste, ground coriander, ground turmeric, and ground white pepper. Cook for another 1-2 minutes until fragrant.
4. Pour in the water and bring the mixture to a boil. Reduce the heat to low and let it simmer for about 30-40 minutes to allow the flavors to develop.
5. Strain the broth through a fine mesh sieve into another pot, pressing down on the solids to extract as much flavor as possible. Discard the solids and return the strained broth to the stove.
6. Season the broth with salt to taste. Keep warm over low heat while you prepare the noodles.
7. Cook the yellow noodles and rice vermicelli noodles in a pot of boiling water according to the package instructions. Drain and set aside.
8. To serve, divide the cooked noodles among serving bowls. Top with blanched bean sprouts, halved hard-boiled eggs, cooked prawns, chopped scallions, and chopped cilantro.
9. Ladle the hot prawn broth over the noodles and garnishes.
10. Serve the Prawn Mee hot with sambal chili paste and lime wedges on the side.
11. Enjoy your flavorful and comforting Prawn Mee soup!

Feel free to customize your Prawn Mee with additional toppings such as sliced fish cakes, fried shallots, or chopped chilies for extra heat. Adjust the seasoning of the broth according to your taste preference.

Otak-Otak

Ingredients:

For the Fish Paste:

- 500g white fish fillets (such as mackerel or tilapia), deboned and skin removed
- 1 cup coconut milk
- 3 tablespoons tapioca flour or cornstarch
- 2 tablespoons fish sauce
- 1 tablespoon sugar
- 2 teaspoons ground turmeric
- 1 teaspoon ground coriander
- 1 teaspoon ground cumin
- 1 teaspoon ground fennel
- 1 teaspoon ground galangal
- 1 teaspoon salt
- 3 kaffir lime leaves, thinly sliced (optional)
- 4-6 red chili peppers, seeded and chopped (adjust to taste)
- 4 shallots, chopped
- 4 cloves garlic, chopped
- 1 lemongrass stalk, white part only, chopped

For Wrapping:

- Banana leaves, cut into rectangles and blanched to soften
- Bamboo skewers or toothpicks, for securing the packets

Instructions:

1. In a food processor or blender, combine all the ingredients for the fish paste. Blend until you get a smooth paste. If the mixture is too thick, you can add a little water to help with blending.
2. Transfer the fish paste to a mixing bowl and mix well to ensure all the ingredients are evenly incorporated.
3. Take a piece of blanched banana leaf and place a spoonful of the fish paste in the center.
4. Fold the banana leaf over the fish paste to form a packet or parcel. Secure the edges with bamboo skewers or toothpicks.
5. Repeat the process with the remaining fish paste and banana leaves.

6. Grill the otak-otak packets over medium heat for about 10-15 minutes on each side until the banana leaves are charred and the fish cake is cooked through.
7. Alternatively, you can steam the otak-otak packets for about 15-20 minutes until cooked through.
8. Once cooked, remove the otak-otak from the grill or steamer and let them cool slightly before serving.
9. To serve, unwrap the banana leaves and enjoy the otak-otak hot as a snack or appetizer.
10. You can also serve otak-otak with steamed rice and a side of sambal chili paste for a delicious meal.
11. Enjoy your homemade otak-otak, bursting with flavors of herbs, spices, and coconut milk!

Feel free to adjust the spiciness of the otak-otak by adding more or fewer chili peppers according to your taste preference. You can also add other ingredients such as lime leaves or turmeric leaves for extra aroma.

Ikan Bakar (Grilled Fish)

Ingredients:

For the Marinade:

- 4 fish fillets (such as red snapper, mackerel, or tilapia)
- 4 tablespoons vegetable oil
- 3 tablespoons soy sauce
- 2 tablespoons lime juice
- 2 tablespoons tamarind paste, dissolved in 1/4 cup warm water
- 2 tablespoons sweet soy sauce (kecap manis)
- 2 cloves garlic, minced
- 1-inch piece ginger, grated
- 2 stalks lemongrass, white part only, minced
- 2 red chili peppers, finely chopped (adjust to taste)
- 1 teaspoon ground turmeric
- 1 teaspoon ground coriander
- 1 teaspoon ground cumin
- 1 teaspoon ground black pepper
- Salt to taste

For Serving:

- Sliced lime or calamansi
- Sambal chili paste
- Fresh herbs (such as cilantro or Thai basil)

Instructions:

1. In a bowl, combine all the ingredients for the marinade: vegetable oil, soy sauce, lime juice, tamarind water, sweet soy sauce, minced garlic, grated ginger, minced lemongrass, chopped red chili peppers, ground turmeric, ground coriander, ground cumin, ground black pepper, and salt. Mix well to combine.
2. Place the fish fillets in a shallow dish or resealable plastic bag. Pour the marinade over the fish, ensuring it is evenly coated. Cover the dish or seal the bag and refrigerate for at least 1 hour, or preferably overnight, to allow the flavors to develop.
3. Preheat your grill to medium-high heat. If using charcoal, wait until the coals are hot and glowing.

4. Remove the fish from the marinade and shake off any excess. Reserve the marinade for basting.
5. Place the fish fillets on the grill, skin-side down, and cook for about 4-5 minutes.
6. Carefully flip the fish using a spatula and cook for an additional 4-5 minutes on the other side, or until the fish is cooked through and easily flakes with a fork. Baste the fish with the reserved marinade occasionally during grilling to keep it moist and flavorful.
7. Once the fish is cooked, remove it from the grill and transfer it to a serving platter.
8. Serve the grilled fish hot, garnished with sliced lime or calamansi and fresh herbs. Accompany it with sambal chili paste on the side for extra flavor and heat.
9. Enjoy your delicious and aromatic Ikan Bakar straight from the grill!

Feel free to adjust the level of spiciness by adding more or fewer chili peppers according to your taste preference. You can also use whole fish instead of fillets if preferred.

Kuih Lapis (Layer Cake)

Ingredients:

For the Batter:

- 400g rice flour
- 200g tapioca flour
- 400g sugar
- 800ml coconut milk
- 1/2 teaspoon salt
- 1/2 teaspoon vanilla extract
- Food coloring (optional), assorted colors

Instructions:

1. In a large mixing bowl, combine the rice flour, tapioca flour, sugar, and salt. Mix well to combine.
2. Gradually add the coconut milk to the dry ingredients, stirring continuously to form a smooth batter. Add the vanilla extract and mix until well incorporated.
3. Divide the batter evenly into separate bowls, depending on how many colors you'd like to use. Add food coloring to each bowl of batter and mix well until the desired colors are achieved.
4. Grease an 8-inch square baking pan or a round pan with a little vegetable oil.
5. Pour a thin layer of one colored batter into the bottom of the greased pan and spread it evenly using a spatula. Steam over medium heat for about 5-7 minutes until the layer is set.
6. Once the first layer is set, pour another thin layer of a different colored batter on top of it. Steam for another 5-7 minutes until set.
7. Continue layering and steaming the batter, alternating colors, until all the batter has been used up. Make sure to press down lightly on each layer to ensure they stick together.
8. Once all the layers are cooked and the final layer is added, steam the kuih lapis for an additional 20-25 minutes, or until fully cooked and firm to the touch.
9. Remove the kuih lapis from the steamer and let it cool completely in the pan.
10. Once cooled, carefully unmold the kuih lapis from the pan and cut it into squares or diamonds.
11. Serve the kuih lapis at room temperature as a delightful sweet snack or dessert.
12. Enjoy your homemade kuih lapis, with its colorful layers and delicious coconut flavor!

Feel free to experiment with different flavors and colors for your kuih lapis. You can also add pandan extract or rose water for extra aroma and flavor.

Nasi Tomato (Tomato Rice)

Ingredients:

- 2 cups long-grain white rice, rinsed and drained
- 2 tablespoons vegetable oil
- 1 onion, finely chopped
- 2 cloves garlic, minced
- 2 tomatoes, chopped
- 1 tablespoon tomato paste
- 1 teaspoon ground turmeric
- 1 teaspoon ground coriander
- 1 teaspoon ground cumin
- 1 teaspoon paprika
- 2 cups chicken or vegetable broth
- Salt to taste
- Chopped fresh cilantro or parsley, for garnish (optional)

Instructions:

1. Heat the vegetable oil in a large pot or saucepan over medium heat. Add the chopped onion and minced garlic, and sauté until softened and fragrant, about 2-3 minutes.
2. Add the chopped tomatoes to the pot and cook until they start to break down and release their juices, about 5 minutes.
3. Stir in the tomato paste, ground turmeric, ground coriander, ground cumin, and paprika. Cook for another 2 minutes, stirring constantly to toast the spices.
4. Add the rinsed and drained rice to the pot, stirring to coat it evenly with the tomato mixture.
5. Pour in the chicken or vegetable broth and season with salt to taste. Stir well to combine.
6. Bring the mixture to a boil, then reduce the heat to low. Cover the pot with a tight-fitting lid and simmer for about 15-20 minutes, or until the rice is cooked and the liquid has been absorbed.
7. Once the rice is cooked, remove the pot from the heat and let it sit, covered, for another 5 minutes to steam.
8. Fluff the rice with a fork and transfer it to a serving dish.
9. Garnish the Nasi Tomato with chopped fresh cilantro or parsley, if desired.

10. Serve the Nasi Tomato hot as a flavorful side dish to accompany your favorite meat or vegetable dishes.
11. Enjoy your delicious and aromatic Tomato Rice!

Feel free to customize the recipe by adding other ingredients such as diced carrots, peas, or bell peppers for extra flavor and texture. You can also adjust the spiciness by adding chopped chili peppers or chili powder according to your taste preference.

Curry Puff

Ingredients:

For the Pastry Dough:

- 2 cups all-purpose flour
- 1/2 teaspoon salt
- 1/2 cup cold butter, cubed
- 1/2 cup cold water

For the Filling:

- 2 large potatoes, peeled and diced
- 1 tablespoon vegetable oil
- 1 onion, finely chopped
- 2 cloves garlic, minced
- 1 tablespoon curry powder
- 1/2 teaspoon ground turmeric
- 1/2 teaspoon ground cumin
- 1/2 teaspoon ground coriander
- 1/2 teaspoon chili powder (optional, adjust to taste)
- Salt to taste
- 200g minced chicken or beef
- 2 tablespoons chopped fresh cilantro (optional)
- 2 hard-boiled eggs, chopped (optional)

For Frying:

- Vegetable oil for deep-frying

Instructions:

1. In a large mixing bowl, combine the all-purpose flour and salt. Add the cold cubed butter and use your fingertips to rub it into the flour until the mixture resembles coarse breadcrumbs.

2. Gradually add the cold water, a little at a time, and mix until a dough forms. Knead the dough lightly until smooth. Cover it with plastic wrap and let it rest in the refrigerator for at least 30 minutes.
3. While the dough is resting, prepare the filling. Boil the diced potatoes in a pot of salted water until tender, then drain and set aside.
4. Heat vegetable oil in a skillet over medium heat. Add the chopped onion and minced garlic, and sauté until softened and fragrant.
5. Add the curry powder, ground turmeric, ground cumin, ground coriander, and chili powder (if using). Stir-fry for 1-2 minutes until the spices are aromatic.
6. Add the minced chicken or beef to the skillet and cook until browned and cooked through. Season with salt to taste.
7. Stir in the boiled diced potatoes and chopped fresh cilantro (if using). Cook for another 2-3 minutes until the mixture is well combined. Remove from heat and let the filling cool slightly.
8. Preheat the oven to 375°F (190°C) if baking the curry puffs.
9. Roll out the chilled pastry dough on a floured surface to about 1/8-inch thickness. Use a round cutter or glass to cut out circles of dough, about 4-5 inches in diameter.
10. Place a spoonful of the filling onto one half of each dough circle. Add a few pieces of chopped hard-boiled egg on top of the filling if desired.
11. Fold the other half of the dough over the filling to create a half-moon shape. Use a fork to press down and seal the edges of the pastry.
12. If deep-frying, heat vegetable oil in a deep fryer or heavy-bottomed pot to 350°F (180°C). Carefully place the curry puffs into the hot oil and fry in batches until golden brown, about 5-7 minutes. Drain on paper towels.
13. If baking, place the assembled curry puffs on a baking sheet lined with parchment paper. Brush the tops with beaten egg for a golden finish. Bake in the preheated oven for 20-25 minutes, or until golden brown.
14. Serve the curry puffs hot or at room temperature as a delicious snack or appetizer.
15. Enjoy your homemade curry puffs, filled with flavorful curry-spiced filling and encased in a crispy pastry crust!

Yong Tau Foo

Ingredients:

For the Fish Paste:

- 300g white fish fillets (such as mackerel or cod), deboned and roughly chopped
- 1 egg white
- 2 tablespoons cornstarch
- 1 tablespoon soy sauce
- 1 teaspoon sesame oil
- 1 teaspoon sugar
- 1/2 teaspoon salt
- 1/4 teaspoon white pepper

For the Stuffing:

- Assorted vegetables and tofu of your choice (such as bell peppers, okra, eggplant, bitter melon, tofu puffs, etc.)

For the Broth (Optional):

- 4 cups chicken or vegetable broth
- 2 slices ginger
- 2 cloves garlic, smashed
- 2 tablespoons soy sauce
- Salt and white pepper to taste

For the Sauce:

- 2 tablespoons soy sauce
- 1 tablespoon oyster sauce
- 1 tablespoon sesame oil
- 1 teaspoon sugar
- 1 clove garlic, minced
- Chili sauce or chopped chili peppers (optional)

Instructions:

1. Prepare the fish paste by blending the white fish fillets in a food processor until smooth. Transfer the fish paste to a mixing bowl and add the egg white, cornstarch, soy sauce, sesame oil, sugar, salt, and white pepper. Mix well until everything is combined and the mixture is smooth.
2. Prepare the vegetables and tofu for stuffing. If using vegetables like bell peppers or bitter melon, cut them in half and remove the seeds. For tofu puffs, cut a slit in the side to form a pocket.
3. Stuff each vegetable or tofu pocket with a generous amount of fish paste, smoothing the surface with a spoon or knife.
4. If making a broth, heat the chicken or vegetable broth in a pot over medium heat. Add the ginger slices, smashed garlic cloves, soy sauce, salt, and white pepper. Let the broth simmer for 10-15 minutes to infuse the flavors.
5. Carefully place the stuffed vegetables and tofu into the simmering broth and let them cook for about 5-7 minutes, or until the fish paste is cooked through and the vegetables are tender.
6. While the yong tau foo is cooking, prepare the sauce by combining soy sauce, oyster sauce, sesame oil, sugar, minced garlic, and chili sauce or chopped chili peppers (if using) in a small bowl.
7. Once the stuffed ingredients are cooked, remove them from the broth using a slotted spoon and arrange them on a serving platter.
8. Serve the yong tau foo hot, either with the clear broth on the side or drizzled with the prepared sauce.
9. Enjoy your homemade yong tau foo as a delicious and satisfying meal or appetizer!

Feel free to customize the ingredients and adjust the seasoning according to your taste preferences. You can also serve yong tau foo with steamed rice or noodles for a more substantial meal.

Kaya Toast

Ingredients:

For the Kaya:

- 4 large eggs
- 200g sugar
- 200ml coconut milk
- 4 pandan leaves, tied into a knot (optional for flavor)
- 1/2 teaspoon vanilla extract

For the Toast:

- Slices of bread (usually white bread or wholemeal bread)
- Butter, softened

Instructions:

1. In a heatproof mixing bowl, whisk together the eggs and sugar until well combined.
2. Stir in the coconut milk and add the pandan leaves (if using).
3. Place the mixing bowl over a pot of simmering water (double boiler method) and cook the mixture, stirring constantly, until it thickens to a custard-like consistency. This will take about 20-30 minutes. Be patient and continue stirring to prevent the mixture from curdling.
4. Once the kaya has thickened, remove the pandan leaves and stir in the vanilla extract. Let the kaya cool completely.
5. While the kaya is cooling, toast the slices of bread until golden brown and crispy.
6. Spread a generous amount of softened butter on one side of each slice of toast.
7. Spoon a generous amount of kaya onto one slice of toast and spread it evenly.
8. Place another slice of toast on top to form a sandwich.
9. Using a sharp knife, cut the sandwich diagonally into halves or quarters.
10. Serve the kaya toast immediately as a delicious breakfast or snack.
11. Enjoy your homemade kaya toast, with its rich and creamy coconut jam filling sandwiched between crispy slices of toast!

Feel free to adjust the sweetness of the kaya according to your taste preference by adding more or less sugar. You can also store any leftover kaya in an airtight container in the refrigerator for up to a week.

Nasi Ulam

Ingredients:

For the Rice:

- 2 cups jasmine rice, rinsed and drained
- 2 cups water

For the Herb and Vegetable Mixture:

- 1 cup finely chopped herbs (such as Thai basil, mint, cilantro, and Vietnamese coriander)
- 1 cup finely shredded vegetables (such as cucumber, carrot, and green beans)
- 1/4 cup finely chopped shallots or red onion
- 1/4 cup finely chopped lemongrass
- 1/4 cup finely chopped torch ginger flower (bunga kantan) (optional)
- 1/4 cup finely chopped kaffir lime leaves
- 1/4 cup finely chopped turmeric leaves (optional)
- 1/4 cup finely chopped laksa leaves (optional)
- 1/4 cup grated coconut, toasted (optional)
- 1/4 cup dried shrimp or anchovies, finely chopped (optional)
- 1/4 cup toasted peanuts, chopped (optional)

For the Seasoning:

- 2 tablespoons fish sauce
- 2 tablespoons lime juice
- 1 tablespoon palm sugar or brown sugar
- 1 tablespoon soy sauce
- 1 tablespoon shrimp paste (belacan), toasted (optional)

For the Sambal (Optional):

- 6-8 red chili peppers, seeded and chopped
- 4 shallots, chopped
- 2 cloves garlic, chopped
- 1 tablespoon shrimp paste (belacan), toasted

- 1 tablespoon tamarind pulp, soaked in 2 tablespoons warm water and strained
- 1 tablespoon palm sugar or brown sugar
- Salt to taste

Instructions:

1. Cook the jasmine rice in a rice cooker or on the stovetop according to package instructions.
2. While the rice is cooking, prepare the herb and vegetable mixture. In a large mixing bowl, combine the finely chopped herbs, shredded vegetables, shallots, lemongrass, torch ginger flower (if using), kaffir lime leaves, turmeric leaves (if using), laksa leaves (if using), grated coconut (if using), dried shrimp or anchovies (if using), and toasted peanuts (if using). Mix well to combine.
3. In a small bowl, mix together the fish sauce, lime juice, palm sugar, soy sauce, and shrimp paste (if using) to make the seasoning.
4. Once the rice is cooked, fluff it with a fork and transfer it to a large serving bowl.
5. Pour the seasoning over the cooked rice and mix well to coat the rice evenly.
6. Add the herb and vegetable mixture to the seasoned rice and toss gently to combine.
7. Taste and adjust the seasoning if necessary, adding more fish sauce, lime juice, or palm sugar as desired.
8. Prepare the sambal, if using, by blending the red chili peppers, shallots, garlic, shrimp paste, tamarind pulp, palm sugar, and salt in a food processor until smooth.
9. Serve the Nasi Ulam immediately with the sambal on the side.
10. Enjoy your homemade Nasi Ulam, a flavorful and aromatic Malaysian dish packed with fresh herbs and vegetables!

Feel free to customize the herb and vegetable mixture according to your taste preferences and the availability of ingredients. You can also add other ingredients such as grated mango or pomelo for extra flavor and texture.

Ais Kacang (Shaved Ice Dessert)

Ingredients:

For the Base:

- 2 cups shaved ice (you can use an ice shaver or crushed ice)
- 2 tablespoons sweetened condensed milk

For the Syrups:

- Red syrup (rose syrup)
- Green syrup (pandan syrup)
- Yellow syrup (such as sweet corn syrup)
- Brown syrup (such as palm sugar syrup or gula Melaka syrup)
- Optional: other flavored syrups like sarsi (sarsaparilla), grass jelly, or cendol syrup

For the Toppings (Optional):

- Red beans, cooked and cooled
- Sweet corn kernels, cooked and cooled
- Grass jelly, cut into cubes
- Cendol (green rice flour jelly)
- Nata de coco (coconut jelly)
- Attap chee (palm seed)
- Chopped peanuts
- Chopped fruit (such as mango, pineapple, or banana)
- A scoop of ice cream (such as vanilla or coconut)

Instructions:

1. Prepare all the toppings by cooking and cooling any ingredients that need to be cooked (such as red beans and sweet corn).
2. Place the shaved ice in a serving bowl or glass.
3. Drizzle the sweetened condensed milk over the shaved ice.
4. Generously pour the various colored syrups over the shaved ice in a decorative pattern. You can create layers of different colors for a vibrant look.

5. Add the toppings of your choice over the syrup-covered shaved ice. Be creative and arrange the toppings in a visually appealing manner.
6. Optional: Add a scoop of ice cream on top for extra indulgence.
7. Serve the Ais Kacang immediately with a long spoon and enjoy!

Ais Kacang is highly customizable, so feel free to adjust the toppings and syrups according to your taste preferences. You can also experiment with different combinations of flavors and textures to create your own unique version of this refreshing dessert.

Bubur Cha Cha (Sweet Potato and Tapioca Dessert)

Ingredients:

- 1 cup sweet potatoes, peeled and cubed
- 1 cup taro, peeled and cubed
- 1/2 cup small tapioca pearls (sago)
- 4 cups water
- 1 pandan leaf, tied into a knot (optional, for flavor)
- 1 can (400ml) coconut milk
- 1/2 cup palm sugar or brown sugar (adjust to taste)
- A pinch of salt

Instructions:

1. In a pot, bring the water to a boil over medium heat. Add the sweet potatoes, taro, and tapioca pearls to the boiling water. Cook until the sweet potatoes, taro, and tapioca pearls are tender, stirring occasionally to prevent sticking, about 15-20 minutes.
2. Once the sweet potatoes, taro, and tapioca pearls are cooked, reduce the heat to low and add the pandan leaf (if using) to infuse flavor. Let it simmer for another 5 minutes.
3. In a separate saucepan, heat the coconut milk over medium heat until warmed through. Do not boil.
4. Add the warmed coconut milk to the pot with the cooked sweet potatoes, taro, and tapioca pearls. Stir to combine.
5. Add the palm sugar or brown sugar to the pot, along with a pinch of salt. Stir until the sugar is dissolved and the bubur cha cha is well combined.
6. Taste and adjust the sweetness according to your preference by adding more sugar if needed.
7. Remove the pandan leaf from the pot before serving.
8. Ladle the bubur cha cha into serving bowls and serve warm.
9. Enjoy your homemade bubur cha cha, a comforting and delicious Malaysian dessert!

You can customize this recipe by adding other ingredients such as yam, pumpkin, or black-eyed peas for additional flavor and texture. Feel free to adjust the consistency of the dessert by adding more or less coconut milk or water according to your preference.

Kuih Talam (Pandan and Coconut Cake)

Ingredients:

For the Pandan Layer:

- 1 cup rice flour
- 1 cup coconut milk
- 1 cup water
- 1/2 cup sugar
- 1/2 teaspoon pandan extract or 4-5 pandan leaves, washed and blended with water, then strained
- A pinch of salt

For the Coconut Layer:

- 1 cup coconut milk
- 2 tablespoons rice flour
- 2 tablespoons tapioca flour or cornstarch
- 3 tablespoons sugar
- A pinch of salt

Instructions:

1. Grease an 8-inch square or round cake pan with a little oil or line it with banana leaves for added flavor (optional).
2. Prepare the pandan layer: In a mixing bowl, combine the rice flour, coconut milk, water, sugar, pandan extract or pandan juice, and a pinch of salt. Mix until smooth and well combined.
3. Pour the pandan mixture into the prepared cake pan, filling it about halfway. Tap the pan gently on the counter to remove any air bubbles.
4. Steam the pandan layer over medium heat for about 10-15 minutes, or until it is set and firm to the touch. Remove the pan from the steamer and set it aside to cool slightly.
5. While the pandan layer is steaming, prepare the coconut layer: In a small saucepan, mix together the coconut milk, rice flour, tapioca flour or cornstarch, sugar, and a pinch of salt. Cook over medium heat, stirring constantly, until the mixture thickens and becomes smooth and glossy, about 5-7 minutes.
6. Pour the coconut layer over the partially cooled pandan layer in the cake pan, spreading it evenly with a spatula.

7. Return the cake pan to the steamer and steam the kuih Talam for another 15-20 minutes, or until the coconut layer is set and firm.
8. Remove the kuih Talam from the steamer and let it cool completely in the pan.
9. Once cooled, slice the kuih Talam into squares or diamonds, and serve at room temperature.
10. Enjoy your homemade kuih Talam, with its delightful combination of pandan and coconut flavors!

Feel free to adjust the sweetness of the kuih Talam by adding more or less sugar according to your taste preferences. You can also experiment with different natural colorings or flavorings for the pandan layer, such as butterfly pea flower extract or pandan paste.

Roti Jala (Lacy Pancakes)

Ingredients:

- 1 cup all-purpose flour
- 1 cup coconut milk
- 1 cup water
- 2 eggs
- 1/2 teaspoon turmeric powder (for color)
- 1/4 teaspoon salt
- Vegetable oil or melted butter, for greasing the pan

Special Equipment:

- Roti Jala mold or funnel with multiple small holes (traditionally, a Roti Jala mold is used, but you can also use a clean, empty ketchup or squeeze bottle with a small nozzle attachment)

Instructions:

1. In a large mixing bowl, combine the all-purpose flour, coconut milk, water, eggs, turmeric powder, and salt. Whisk until the batter is smooth and free of lumps. The consistency should be similar to that of crepe batter, thin enough to pour but not too runny.
2. Heat a non-stick skillet or crepe pan over medium heat and lightly grease it with vegetable oil or melted butter.
3. Pour a small amount of the batter into the Roti Jala mold or funnel, filling it about halfway.
4. Holding the mold or funnel over the heated skillet, move it in a circular motion to create a lacy net pattern with the batter. Start from the center and work your way outward, overlapping the lines slightly.
5. Cook the Roti Jala for about 1-2 minutes, or until the edges start to lift and the bottom is lightly golden brown.
6. Carefully loosen the edges of the Roti Jala with a spatula and gently lift it from the pan. Fold it in half or roll it up loosely, and transfer it to a serving plate.
7. Repeat the process with the remaining batter, greasing the pan lightly between each Roti Jala to prevent sticking.
8. Serve the Roti Jala warm with your favorite curry or spicy dish for dipping.
9. Enjoy your homemade Roti Jala, with its delicate lacy texture and fragrant aroma!

Roti Jala is best served fresh and warm, but you can also make it ahead of time and reheat it gently in the microwave or steamer before serving. Feel free to experiment with different fillings or toppings for your Roti Jala, such as shredded chicken, beef, or vegetables.

Laksam

Ingredients:

For the Rice Noodles:

- 500g rice flour
- 2 cups water
- Salt, to taste

For the Coconut Milk Gravy:

- 400ml coconut milk
- 2 cups water
- 3 tablespoons fish or chicken stock powder
- 2 tablespoons rice flour, mixed with 3 tablespoons water to make a slurry
- 1 stalk lemongrass, bruised
- 2 kaffir lime leaves
- Salt, to taste

For the Garnish:

- 1 cucumber, julienned
- 1 carrot, julienned
- 1 cup bean sprouts, blanched
- 1 cup shredded cabbage, blanched
- Hard-boiled eggs, sliced (optional)
- Fresh herbs such as Vietnamese mint (daun kesum) or cilantro, chopped

Instructions:

1. Prepare the rice noodles: In a large mixing bowl, combine the rice flour, water, and salt to form a smooth batter.
2. Heat a non-stick pan over medium heat and lightly grease it with oil. Pour a ladleful of the batter onto the pan, tilting the pan to spread the batter thinly and evenly. Cook until the edges of the noodle sheet start to curl and lift from the pan. Remove the noodle sheet from the pan and repeat the process with the

remaining batter. Once cooled, roll up the noodle sheets and slice them into thin strips. Set aside.
3. Prepare the coconut milk gravy: In a pot, combine the coconut milk, water, fish or chicken stock powder, lemongrass, and kaffir lime leaves. Bring to a gentle simmer over medium heat.
4. Gradually stir in the rice flour slurry, stirring constantly to prevent lumps from forming. Cook for 2-3 minutes until the gravy thickens slightly. Season with salt to taste.
5. To serve, arrange the sliced rice noodles in serving bowls. Ladle the hot coconut milk gravy over the noodles.
6. Garnish with julienned cucumber, carrot, blanched bean sprouts, shredded cabbage, and sliced hard-boiled eggs (if using).
7. Sprinkle chopped fresh herbs over the top for added flavor and freshness.
8. Serve the Laksam immediately while hot, with additional chili paste or sambal on the side for those who prefer a spicier kick.
9. Enjoy your homemade Laksam, a comforting and flavorful Malaysian noodle dish!

Laksam is traditionally enjoyed as a hearty breakfast or brunch dish, but it can be served at any time of the day as a satisfying meal. Feel free to customize the garnishes and adjust the level of spiciness according to your taste preferences.

Bubur Pulut Hitam (Black Glutinous Rice Porridge)

Ingredients:

- 1 cup black glutinous rice (pulut hitam)
- 6 cups water
- 1 pandan leaf, tied into a knot (optional, for added flavor)
- 1 cup coconut milk
- 1/2 cup palm sugar or brown sugar (adjust to taste)
- A pinch of salt

Optional Garnishes:

- Coconut milk, for drizzling
- Toasted coconut flakes
- Additional palm sugar or brown sugar, for extra sweetness

Instructions:

1. Rinse the black glutinous rice under cold water until the water runs clear. Drain well.
2. In a large pot, combine the rinsed black glutinous rice, water, and pandan leaf (if using). Bring to a boil over medium-high heat.
3. Once boiling, reduce the heat to low and let the rice simmer, partially covered, for about 1 to 1.5 hours, or until the grains are tender and the mixture has thickened. Stir occasionally to prevent sticking and burning. You may need to add more water if the mixture becomes too thick before the rice is fully cooked.
4. Once the rice is cooked and the mixture has thickened to your desired consistency, remove the pandan leaf from the pot.
5. Stir in the coconut milk, palm sugar or brown sugar, and a pinch of salt. Continue to cook for another 5-10 minutes, stirring occasionally, until the sugar is fully dissolved and the porridge is thick and creamy.
6. Taste and adjust the sweetness according to your preference by adding more sugar if desired.
7. Once the porridge reaches your desired consistency and sweetness, remove it from the heat.
8. Ladle the Bubur Pulut Hitam into serving bowls.

9. Garnish each bowl with a drizzle of coconut milk and a sprinkle of toasted coconut flakes, if desired.
10. Serve the Bubur Pulut Hitam warm or at room temperature.
11. Enjoy your homemade Bubur Pulut Hitam, a comforting and flavorful Malaysian dessert!

Feel free to adjust the sweetness of the porridge according to your taste preferences by adding more or less sugar. You can also experiment with different garnishes such as chopped nuts or dried fruits for added texture and flavor.

Soto Ayam (Chicken Soup)

Ingredients:

For the Soup:

- 1 whole chicken (about 1.5 kg), cut into pieces
- 2 liters water
- 3 stalks lemongrass, bruised
- 5 kaffir lime leaves
- 3 Indonesian bay leaves (daun salam)
- 3 cloves garlic, minced
- 1 thumb-sized piece of ginger, sliced
- 1 thumb-sized piece of galangal, sliced
- 1 teaspoon ground turmeric
- 1 teaspoon ground coriander
- 1 teaspoon ground cumin
- Salt, to taste
- Sugar, to taste
- Lime juice, to taste

For the Spice Paste (Bumbu):

- 6 shallots, peeled
- 4 cloves garlic, peeled
- 2 thumb-sized pieces of ginger, peeled
- 2 thumb-sized pieces of fresh turmeric, peeled (or 1 tablespoon ground turmeric)
- 3-4 candlenuts or macadamia nuts (optional)
- 2 teaspoons ground coriander
- 1 teaspoon ground cumin
- 1 teaspoon ground white pepper
- 1 teaspoon shrimp paste (terasi or belacan)

For Serving:

- Cooked rice or vermicelli noodles
- Hard-boiled eggs, halved
- Fried shallots (bawang goreng)
- Fresh cilantro leaves
- Lime wedges

- Sambal or chili sauce (optional)

Instructions:

1. Prepare the spice paste (bumbu): In a food processor or blender, blend together the shallots, garlic, ginger, turmeric, candlenuts (if using), ground coriander, ground cumin, ground white pepper, and shrimp paste until smooth. Set aside.
2. In a large pot, bring the water to a boil over medium-high heat. Add the chicken pieces, lemongrass, kaffir lime leaves, Indonesian bay leaves, minced garlic, sliced ginger, galangal, ground turmeric, ground coriander, and ground cumin.
3. Lower the heat to medium-low and let the soup simmer gently, uncovered, for about 30-45 minutes, or until the chicken is cooked through and tender.
4. Remove the chicken pieces from the pot and set aside to cool slightly. Once cool enough to handle, shred the chicken meat into bite-sized pieces and discard the bones and skin. Return the shredded chicken meat to the pot.
5. Add the spice paste (bumbu) to the pot and stir well to combine. Season the soup with salt, sugar, and lime juice to taste. Continue to simmer the soup for another 10-15 minutes to allow the flavors to meld.
6. To serve, place a portion of cooked rice or vermicelli noodles in serving bowls. Ladle the hot Soto Ayam over the rice or noodles. Garnish with hard-boiled eggs, fried shallots, fresh cilantro leaves, and lime wedges. Serve with sambal or chili sauce on the side, if desired.
7. Enjoy your homemade Soto Ayam, a comforting and flavorful Indonesian chicken soup!

Feel free to customize the toppings and garnishes according to your taste preferences. You can also add other ingredients such as potato or cabbage to the soup for extra texture and flavor.

Ketupat

Ingredients:

- 2 cups glutinous rice
- 4-5 pieces of coconut leaves or banana leaves (each about 12 inches long)
- Salt, to taste

Instructions:

1. Rinse the glutinous rice under cold water until the water runs clear. Drain well.
2. Soak the glutinous rice in water for at least 2 hours or overnight.
3. While the rice is soaking, prepare the pouches for the Ketupat. If you're using coconut leaves, remove the center rib from each leaf to make them more pliable. Cut the leaves into rectangular pieces, about 12 inches long and 6 inches wide. If you're using banana leaves, cut them into similar-sized pieces and pass them over an open flame briefly to soften them.
4. Fold each piece of leaf into a triangular cone, overlapping the edges to form a pouch. Secure the edges with toothpicks or staples to hold the pouch together.
5. Drain the soaked glutinous rice and divide it evenly among the leaf pouches, filling them about three-quarters full. Add a pinch of salt to each pouch to season the rice.
6. Fold the tops of the leaf pouches down to cover the rice, then fold the sides inward to seal the pouch completely.
7. Use kitchen twine to tie the pouches securely, making sure they are tightly sealed to prevent the rice from escaping during cooking.
8. Fill a large pot with water and bring it to a boil over medium-high heat. Carefully add the Ketupat pouches to the boiling water, making sure they are fully submerged.
9. Reduce the heat to low and let the Ketupat simmer gently for about 4-6 hours, depending on the size of the pouches. Make sure to check the water level periodically and add more boiling water as needed to keep the Ketupat submerged.
10. Once cooked, remove the Ketupat pouches from the pot and let them cool slightly.
11. Carefully unwrap the leaf pouches from the Ketupat and discard them. Cut the Ketupat into slices or cubes and serve warm or at room temperature.
12. Enjoy your homemade Ketupat with traditional accompaniments such as rendang, sambal, or peanut sauce.

Ketupat can be stored in the refrigerator for up to a week or frozen for longer storage. If freezing, make sure to thaw the Ketupat completely before reheating.

Pulut Panggang (Grilled Glutinous Rice)

Ingredients:

For the Glutinous Rice:

- 2 cups glutinous rice, soaked overnight
- 1 cup thick coconut milk
- 1 teaspoon salt

For the Filling:

- 200g shredded cooked chicken or beef (you can also use shredded fish or shrimp)
- 1 large onion, finely chopped
- 3 cloves garlic, minced
- 2 tablespoons vegetable oil
- 1 teaspoon ground turmeric
- 1 teaspoon ground coriander
- 1 teaspoon ground cumin
- Salt and pepper, to taste

For Assembly:

- Banana leaves, cut into 6-inch squares and wilted over an open flame
- Toothpicks or bamboo skewers, for securing the parcels

Instructions:

1. Prepare the glutinous rice: Drain the soaked glutinous rice and rinse it under cold water until the water runs clear. Drain well.
2. In a large bowl, combine the glutinous rice, coconut milk, and salt. Mix well to ensure the rice is evenly coated. Set aside to marinate for at least 30 minutes.
3. Prepare the filling: Heat the vegetable oil in a pan over medium heat. Add the chopped onion and minced garlic, and sauté until softened and fragrant, about 2-3 minutes.
4. Add the shredded chicken or beef to the pan, along with the ground turmeric, ground coriander, and ground cumin. Season with salt and pepper to taste. Cook, stirring occasionally, until the filling is heated through and the flavors are well combined. Remove from heat and set aside to cool slightly.

5. To assemble the Pulut Panggang, place a spoonful of the marinated glutinous rice onto the center of a piece of wilted banana leaf. Flatten the rice slightly to form a small rectangle or square.
6. Spoon a portion of the filling onto the center of the rice, then fold the sides of the banana leaf over the filling to enclose it completely. Secure the parcel with toothpicks or bamboo skewers.
7. Repeat the process with the remaining glutinous rice and filling until all the parcels are assembled.
8. Preheat a grill or oven to medium-high heat.
9. Place the Pulut Panggang parcels on the grill or on a baking sheet lined with banana leaves. Grill or bake for about 15-20 minutes, or until the banana leaves are charred and the rice is cooked through.
10. Carefully remove the Pulut Panggang from the grill or oven and let them cool slightly before serving.
11. Serve the Pulut Panggang warm as a snack or appetizer. Enjoy the fragrant aroma and delicious flavors of this traditional Malaysian and Indonesian dish!

You can customize the filling according to your preferences by using different proteins such as fish, shrimp, or tofu, and adding additional vegetables or spices. Feel free to experiment with different combinations to create your own unique Pulut Panggang recipe.

Cendol

Ingredients:

For the Cendol:

- 100g rice flour
- 50g tapioca flour
- 1 tablespoon pandan extract or pandan paste
- 200ml water
- Ice water (for rinsing the cendol)

For the Coconut Milk:

- 400ml coconut milk
- 100ml water
- 50g palm sugar or brown sugar
- A pinch of salt

For Serving (Optional):

- Cooked red beans
- Cooked sweet corn kernels
- Grass jelly, cut into cubes
- Crushed ice

Instructions:

1. Prepare the Cendol:
    - In a mixing bowl, combine the rice flour, tapioca flour, pandan extract or pandan paste, and water. Mix until smooth and well combined.
    - Transfer the batter to a fine-mesh sieve or a colander with small holes.
    - Hold the sieve or colander over a pot of boiling water. Using a spatula or spoon, press the batter through the holes to form thin strands directly into the boiling water. Cook for about 2-3 minutes, stirring occasionally.
    - Once the cendol noodles are cooked, transfer them to a bowl of ice water to cool. This will stop the cooking process and give the cendol its characteristic chewy texture. Drain well and set aside.

2. Prepare the Coconut Milk:
    - In a saucepan, combine the coconut milk, water, palm sugar or brown sugar, and a pinch of salt. Stir over medium heat until the sugar is dissolved and the mixture is heated through. Do not boil.
    - Remove from heat and let the coconut milk mixture cool slightly.
3. To Serve:
    - Place a portion of the cooked cendol noodles in serving bowls.
    - Pour the coconut milk mixture over the cendol noodles.
    - Add cooked red beans, sweet corn kernels, and grass jelly cubes as desired.
    - If preferred, add crushed ice to the bowls to make the dessert extra refreshing.
    - Serve the cendol immediately and enjoy!

Cendol is best enjoyed fresh, but you can also store any leftover cendol noodles in the refrigerator for a day or two. Simply reheat them in hot water before serving. Feel free to customize your cendol with your favorite toppings and adjust the sweetness of the coconut milk according to your taste preferences.

Mee Jawa

Ingredients:

For the Gravy:

- 2 tablespoons vegetable oil
- 3 shallots, finely chopped
- 3 cloves garlic, minced
- 1 inch ginger, minced
- 2 tablespoons chili paste (adjust to taste)
- 2 tomatoes, diced
- 1 tablespoon tamarind paste dissolved in 1 cup of water
- 2 tablespoons sweet soy sauce (kecap manis)
- 1 tablespoon soy sauce
- 1 tablespoon palm sugar or brown sugar (adjust to taste)
- Salt to taste

For the Noodles and Toppings:

- 300g yellow noodles, blanched
- 100g firm tofu, cubed and fried
- 1 small potato, boiled and cubed
- 2 hard-boiled eggs, halved
- Bean sprouts, blanched
- Fried shallots for garnish
- Chopped cilantro or spring onions for garnish
- Lime wedges for serving

Instructions:

1. Heat the vegetable oil in a large pot or wok over medium heat. Add the shallots, garlic, and ginger, and sauté until fragrant.
2. Add the chili paste and continue to sauté for another minute until the spices are well combined.
3. Add the diced tomatoes and cook until they start to soften.
4. Pour in the tamarind water, sweet soy sauce, regular soy sauce, and palm sugar. Stir well to combine and bring the mixture to a simmer.

5. Let the gravy simmer for about 10-15 minutes until it thickens slightly and the flavors meld together. Adjust the seasoning with salt and additional sugar or soy sauce if needed.
6. While the gravy is simmering, prepare the noodles and toppings. Blanch the yellow noodles and bean sprouts in boiling water until cooked, then drain well.
7. Arrange the blanched noodles, tofu, boiled potato, and hard-boiled eggs in serving bowls.
8. Ladle the hot gravy over the noodles and toppings.
9. Garnish with fried shallots and chopped cilantro or spring onions.
10. Serve the Mee Jawa hot with lime wedges on the side for squeezing over the noodles.
11. Enjoy your homemade Mee Jawa, a delicious and comforting noodle dish packed with flavor!

Feel free to customize the toppings according to your preference. You can also add additional ingredients such as shrimp, chicken, or fried shallots for extra flavor. Adjust the spiciness of the gravy by adding more or less chili paste according to your taste preference.

Nasi Lemuni

Ingredients:

- 2 cups jasmine rice
- 3 cups water
- A handful of Lemuni leaves (can substitute with lemon basil or regular basil leaves)
- Salt, to taste

Instructions:

1. Rinse the jasmine rice under cold water until the water runs clear. Drain well.
2. In a rice cooker or pot, combine the rinsed rice and water.
3. Add the Lemuni leaves to the rice and water mixture. You can tear the leaves slightly to release more flavor.
4. Season with salt to taste.
5. If using a rice cooker, cook the rice according to the manufacturer's instructions. If using a pot, bring the rice mixture to a boil over medium-high heat, then reduce the heat to low, cover, and simmer for about 15-20 minutes, or until the rice is cooked and all the water has been absorbed.
6. Once the rice is cooked, fluff it with a fork to mix in the Lemuni leaves evenly.
7. Serve the Nasi Lemuni hot as a side dish to accompany your favorite Indonesian dishes.
8. Enjoy the fragrant and aromatic flavors of Nasi Lemuni!

Nasi Lemuni is typically served as a side dish alongside other Indonesian dishes such as grilled meats, curries, or stir-fries. The Lemuni leaves impart a subtle citrusy fragrance to the rice, adding a unique twist to your meal. If Lemuni leaves are not available, you can use lemon basil or regular basil leaves as a substitute, although the flavor may differ slightly.

Sambal Belacan

Ingredients:

- 10-12 red chili peppers (use fewer for a milder sambal)
- 1 teaspoon shrimp paste (belacan)
- 2 cloves garlic
- 2 shallots
- 1 tablespoon lime juice
- 1 teaspoon sugar
- Salt, to taste

Instructions:

1. Begin by preparing the chili peppers. Remove the stems and cut them into smaller pieces. If you prefer a milder sambal, you can remove the seeds and membranes from the chili peppers.
2. In a mortar and pestle, grind the shrimp paste (belacan) until it forms a smooth paste. Alternatively, you can wrap the belacan in aluminum foil and roast it over an open flame until fragrant.
3. Add the garlic cloves and shallots to the mortar and pestle, and pound them into a rough paste along with the shrimp paste.
4. Add the chopped chili peppers to the mortar and continue pounding until they are well combined with the other ingredients and form a coarse paste. Alternatively, you can use a food processor to blend the ingredients into a paste.
5. Transfer the chili paste to a bowl and add lime juice, sugar, and salt to taste. Mix well to combine.
6. Taste the sambal and adjust the seasoning if needed, adding more lime juice, sugar, or salt according to your preference.
7. Let the sambal sit for at least 15-20 minutes to allow the flavors to meld together.
8. Serve the Sambal Belacan as a condiment alongside your favorite Malaysian or Indonesian dishes. It pairs well with grilled meats, seafood, rice, noodles, and more.
9. Store any leftover sambal in an airtight container in the refrigerator for up to a week. The flavors will continue to develop over time, making it even more delicious with age.

Enjoy the spicy, savory, and tangy flavors of homemade Sambal Belacan! Adjust the quantity of chili peppers according to your preferred level of spiciness, and feel free to experiment with additional ingredients such as tamarind pulp, ginger, or lemongrass for added complexity.

Mee Bandung Muar

Ingredients:

For the Broth:

- 500g prawns, shells removed and deveined (reserve some for garnish)
- 500g beef, cut into cubes
- 2 liters water
- 1 onion, chopped
- 3 cloves garlic, minced
- 2 tomatoes, chopped
- 2 tablespoons tomato paste
- 2 tablespoons chili paste (adjust to taste)
- 1 tablespoon tamarind paste
- 2 tablespoons palm sugar or brown sugar
- Salt and pepper to taste

For the Noodles and Toppings:

- 400g yellow noodles, blanched
- Fried tofu cubes
- Fried shallots
- Bean sprouts, blanched
- Hard-boiled eggs, halved
- Lime wedges
- Chopped cilantro or spring onions for garnish

Instructions:

1. In a large pot, bring the water to a boil over medium-high heat. Add the prawn shells and beef cubes to the pot and simmer for about 30 minutes to extract the flavors.
2. Strain the broth, discarding the prawn shells and keeping the beef cubes. Return the broth to the pot.
3. Add the chopped onion, minced garlic, chopped tomatoes, tomato paste, chili paste, tamarind paste, and palm sugar to the pot. Stir well to combine.
4. Bring the broth back to a simmer and let it cook for another 15-20 minutes until the flavors meld together and the broth thickens slightly. Season with salt and pepper to taste.

5. While the broth is simmering, prepare the toppings. Blanch the bean sprouts and set aside.
6. To serve, divide the blanched yellow noodles into serving bowls. Top with fried tofu cubes, fried shallots, blanched bean sprouts, hard-boiled eggs, and reserved prawns.
7. Ladle the hot broth over the noodles and toppings.
8. Garnish with chopped cilantro or spring onions and serve immediately with lime wedges on the side.
9. Enjoy your homemade Mee Bandung Muar, a delicious and hearty noodle dish packed with flavor!

Feel free to customize the toppings according to your preference. You can also adjust the spiciness of the broth by adding more or less chili paste. Mee Bandung Muar is typically served as a main dish for lunch or dinner, but you can enjoy it any time of the day.

Sambal Goreng

Ingredients:

- 200g tofu, cut into cubes
- 200g tempeh, cut into cubes
- 2 tablespoons vegetable oil
- 4 shallots, thinly sliced
- 3 cloves garlic, minced
- 2 red chilies, thinly sliced
- 2 green chilies, thinly sliced
- 3 kaffir lime leaves, thinly sliced
- 2 tablespoons tamarind paste
- 2 tablespoons sweet soy sauce (kecap manis)
- Salt and sugar to taste

Instructions:

1. Heat the vegetable oil in a large pan over medium heat. Fry the tofu and tempeh cubes until golden brown and crispy. Remove from the pan and set aside.
2. In the same pan, add a little more oil if needed. Sauté the shallots, garlic, red chilies, green chilies, and kaffir lime leaves until fragrant.
3. Add the tamarind paste and sweet soy sauce to the pan. Stir well to combine.
4. Return the fried tofu and tempeh to the pan. Stir-fry until the tofu and tempeh are evenly coated with the sauce.
5. Season with salt and sugar to taste, adjusting the seasoning as needed.
6. Continue to cook for another 2-3 minutes, allowing the flavors to meld together.
7. Remove from heat and transfer the Sambal Goreng to a serving dish.
8. Serve hot as a side dish or accompaniment to rice or other Indonesian dishes.
9. Enjoy your homemade Sambal Goreng, packed with spicy, savory flavors!

Feel free to customize the Sambal Goreng according to your preference by adjusting the amount of chili for spiciness or adding other ingredients like diced tomatoes or green beans for extra texture and flavor.

www.ingramcontent.com/pod-product-compliance
Lightning Source LLC
LaVergne TN
LVHW061944070526
838199LV00060B/3959